Magic Spices

200 Healthy Recipes
Featuring
30 Common Spices

D1529763

Donna L. Weihofen
R.D., M.S.

JOHN WILEY & SONS, INC.

New York • Chichester • Weinheim • Brisbane • Singapore • Toronto

Copyright © 1998 by Donna L. Weihofen, R.D., M.S.
All rights reserved
Published by John Wiley & Sons, Inc.
Published simultaneously in Canada
Previously published by Chronimed Publishing

The information contained in this book is not intended to
serve as a replacement for professional medical advice.
Any use of the information in this book is at the reader's
discretion. The author and the publisher specifically
disclaim any and all liability arising directly or indirectly
from the use or application of any information contained in
this book. A health care professional should be consulted
regarding your specific situation.

Library of Congress Cataloging-in-Publication Data:

10 9 8 7 6 5

The spices used to create the great-tasting and easy-to-prepare recipes found in this book will add a new richness to your food. This book was inspired by my desire to prepare unique and flavorful meals that are also fast, simple, and sensibly low in fat. With only 30 spices, you can take ordinary dishes and make them extraordinary.

Just as spices have added zest to my food, my friends and loving family have added zest and enjoyment to my life. I would like to thank my patient and loving husband, Ray, along with my talented and supportive children, Wayne, Wendy, and Vicki. Their encouragement and understanding helped make my visions for this book a reality. The very biggest thank-you goes to my lifelong friend Mary Risgaard, who served as my extraordinary recipe tester. Her practical suggestions were invaluable in perfecting these recipes.

Thank you also to the wonderful Penzeys stores in Madison and Brookfield, Wisconsin, which specialize in exceptional spices and seasonings. Just walking into the aromatic store was an inspiration for this book.

I hope that the recipes in this book will spice up your life. Enjoy the taste adventure!

Introduction

This book is written to help you spice up your life by adding zest to your cooking, without complicating your life. It doesn't take hundreds of spices and a degree from a cooking school. Just 30 spices will provide plenty of variety, but you can start out with 20 and build your collection.

Spices will bring a new richness to your food and put you in touch with your ancestors from centuries past. Spices have been used as long as man has walked the earth and eaten plants to survive. Men and women learned to eat plants that kept them alive and didn't make them sick. They also learned to eat plants to help them feel better when they developed an ailment. Some of those plants are what we identify today as spices and herbs.

Spices are the fragrant parts of certain tropical and temperate-zone plants. Spices are dried to retain their fragrance and flavor. Parts of the plants used for spicing up our food include the bark as in cinnamon, the bud as in cloves, the berry as in allspice, the flower stigma as in saffron, the kernel or nut as in nutmeg, the seed as in cardamom, and even the rhizome or root as in ginger.

Herbs are the leaves or tender stems of plants that are fragrant such as oregano, thyme, basil, rosemary, parsley, and cilantro. Herbs can be used fresh or dried. Since herbs are just another part of the plant, you don't have to make a big distinction between what is a spice and what is an herb. For the purpose of this book, they will all be referred to as spices.

Spices have been used for hundreds of centuries to enhance health and vitality, and to prevent plague and disease. They have been used as home remedies to help everything from bad breath to intestinal gas to improving sexual vitality. They have also been used as cleaning agents, dyes, cosmetics, and potpourri mixtures and even for decorative craft projects.

Spices are readily available to us, but there was a time when spices were the most valued trade items in the world. Most of the spices were indigenous to China and they were transported into India, Arabia, and Egypt by camel caravans over treacherous terrain. To satisfy the European desire and demand for these exotic flavors, ships were sent out to find new routes to the East. It was in search of a new sea route to the East that Columbus discovered America. When spices were being transported and traded in those days, they were as valuable as gold. The punishment for those who adulterated or stole spices was death.

Common questions about cooking with spices

What makes spices smell and taste so good?

The fragrance and taste of a plant comes from substances called essential oils that are carried in the cells of the plant's tissue. Sometimes these substances are spread throughout the plant but more often they are concentrated in just one part. These oils are made up of various chemical substances, which is one reason we describe their taste as complex. And many of the chemicals are present in more than one spice, although not usually in the same proportion. Imitation flavors are produced in the laboratory in an attempt to put together the right combination of chemicals, but they never quite capture the wonderful aroma and tastes of nature's best.

Is it better to buy the whole spice rather than the ground spice?

It would be ideal to buy many of the spices as they come from the plant and grind or grate them as you need them because the essential oils in the plant remain undisturbed if the spice remains intact. Essential oils are volatile, meaning they will eventually evaporate. To release

the oils that are in the spices, the cell walls must be ruptured. In whole spices, the essential oils are locked into the interior and there they will stay until they meet up with a grater or grinder. Once spices are ground, the entire plant structure is exposed to air, and the process of evaporation begins.

It is not always practical to grate or grind the spices yourself, so spices are available in the powdered or processed form. For most of your recipes, that will work just fine. There are a few spices, however, such as nutmeg and pepper, that you will want to keep on hand in the whole form and freshly grind or grate them when you need them.

What kind of grinders are needed?

A simple mortar and pestle has served cooks since prehistoric times. It works well to crush seeds and leaves. A good pepper grinder is one of those essential kitchen utensils that will enhance your cooking. Freshly ground pepper is truly superior to pepper in the shaker. For nutmeg, you can use a small inexpensive nutmeg grater.

Are there any special ways to store spices?

All ground and whole spices should be kept in a dark, cool part of your kitchen. The worst spot is right above the stove. Keep them in airtight containers. Glass jars work best because you can also see the spice.

How long do they last?

If spices are stored properly they will last for years, especially if they are whole. Some seeds, such as mustard seeds and sesame seeds, may become rancid unless stored in the refrigerator but most others are fine at a cool room temperature. Ground spices may loose some potency if kept a long time but that doesn't mean you have to throw them out. Just use a little more if the spice has been around a while.

Are there any rules to help with how much of a spice to use in recipes?

The amount of a spice to use is a matter of taste. Spices should improve the flavor of a food and make even the simplest foods more delicious and special. If the right amount is used, the result is a delicately subtle one, and the natural flavor of the food is not smothered by too much seasoning. However, there is not one right amount to use. The perfect flavor for you may not be the perfect flavor for another. But that is where the joy of experimenting and discovering new flavors comes in. Just start with very small amounts and add more to suit your taste. You can always add a little more but once you've put it in the dish, you can't take it out.

Some general guidelines

Add whole spices to your recipe if you want the texture, but remember that some whole spices can be very unpleasant to eat. If you would like the flavor without pieces of spice in the dish, use the ground spice.

If you would like to use a fresh herb but the recipe calls for a dried herb, such as dried tarragon, use three times more of the fresh. (For example, use 3 teaspoons of fresh tarragon for 1 teaspoon of dried tarragon.) Dried seasonings are added in the beginning of the food preparation but fresh herbs are often added toward the end of the cooking process.

Herbs can be preserved by drying. Wash fresh unwilted leaves. To air-dry, tie a bunch of stems together with a string. Hang upside down in a warm, dry place away from direct sunlight. Make sure the

air is dry and can circulate to prevent mildew from forming. Herbs can also be dried in a warm oven.

Dried herbs will develop a better aromatic quality if the herbs are warmed in hot butter or steeped in a hot liquid for a few minutes before they are added to a recipe.

It is best not to season every dish of a meal with the same spice.

The golden rule when cooking with spices is, "When in doubt, add less." A little bit can provide a subtle, pleasing flavor, but using too much seasoning can overwhelm your dish. If you are unsure if you will like a particular spice or spice combination, err on the side of using too little and adding more to suit your taste. You can always add more, but when you add too much, you can not take it out. When doubling recipes, it may work better not to double all the spices. Try one-and-a-half times the spices for a doubled recipe.

Be adventuresome and experiment with spices in your everyday cooking. It can add zest to your life.

International flavor flair

Some seasoning combinations reflect traditional flavors. Try some of the following ingredient combinations to add international flavoring to your cooking:

Caribbean
Allspice, cloves, ginger, rum, lime, mangoes, bananas

French
Tarragon, thyme, wine, white beans

Italian
Garlic, oregano, basil, rosemary, crushed red pepper, tomatoes

Greek/Mediterranean

Rosemary, oregano, paprika, cinnamon, dill weed, garlic, olive oil, lemon

Mexican

Cumin, cayenne pepper, chili powder, cilantro, garlic, chiles, corn, red beans

Oriental

Ginger, crushed red pepper, whole red chiles, white pepper, soy sauce, garlic

Russian

Paprika, onion, cucumber, sour cream

Southwestern

Cumin, chiles, garlic, onion, corn, black beans

Thai

Ginger, basil, cinnamon, turmeric, cilantro, hot peppers, crushed red pepper, lime, peanuts, coconut milk

Notes about this book

All spices and seasonings in the recipes are dried unless specified "fresh." For example, if the recipe calls for "basil," assume it is dried basil.

All ingredients in the recipes are generally available in large supermarkets. There is no need to go to specialty or health food stores.

Most of the recipes are low in fat and healthy food choices. In order to compensate for fat and still prepare great tasting lower-fat foods, the recipes call for a combination of spices and herbs. As you use spices more often, experiment with other combinations and create your own unique-tasting dishes.

The calories and nutrient information for each recipe are derived from a computer analysis (Master Cook 4.0-Sierra Home) based on information from the USDA. Every effort has been made to check the accuracy of these numbers. It is important, however, to note that there are numerous variables in making these calculations. All analyses should be considered approximate.

Fiber content of each recipe is listed as low (less than 1 gram per serving), medium (1–3 grams per serving), high (3–4 grams per serving), or very high (more than 4 grams per serving). Measurement of fiber is not an exact science. In fact measuring the amount of fiber in food can vary as much as 50 percent from one research report to another, depending on the method of analysis used. Dietary fiber contains the parts of plant materials that are resistant to human digestive enzymes. Dietary fiber is considered to be the sum of indigestible carbohydrate and carbohydrate-like components of foods. Cereal grains, vegetables, fruits, legumes, seeds, and nuts are the major sources of dietary fiber. Processing these foods, such as grinding or cooking, can affect the physical properties of the food, but the fiber remains.

References

Hayes, W. *Spices and Herbs—Lore & Cookery*, Dover Publications, New York, 1980.

Miloradovich and Watson, *Cooking with Herbs and Spices*, Dover Publications, New York, 1950, renewed 1977.

Norman, J. *The Complete Book of Spices—A practical guide to spices & aromatic seeds*, Viking Studio Books, New York, 1990.

Penzeys, Ltd.—exceptional spices and seasonings available through a mail-order catalog. P.O. Box 933, Muskego, WI 53150 (414/679-7207).

Sahni, J. *Savoring Spices and Herbs*, William Morrow and Company, New York, 1996.

Stuckey, M. *The Complete Spice Book with 200 Delicious Recipes plus Potpourris, Beauty Secrets, Health Tips and More!* St. Martin's Press. New York, 1997.

The Top 20 Spices

Allspice

Naming a spice "allspice" seems to imply that it is a blend of many spices. Allspice, however, is a real spice with its own identity. It probably acquired its name because it has the aroma and taste of cinnamon, cloves, and nutmeg, all wrapped into one pea-shaped berry.

Allspice comes from the fruit of a beautiful evergreen tree that is grown in Jamaica, Mexico, and South America. Jamaica has, by far, the largest plantations of these trees. In fact, the trees were growing in Jamaica when Christopher Columbus landed there in search of spices, but he did not recognize this particular berry as a spice.

History records that the Mayans and the Aztecs used the allspice berry in drinks. It was also used to preserve meat and as an embalming spice. It has a wonderful aroma, and today it is used in some spice-based perfumes, in spice-filled hot pads and in potpourri mixtures.

Allspice can be purchased as whole, dried berries where most of the flavor is in the outer shell rather than in the seed inside. The berries are green when picked but when dried they turn a reddish brown color. The berries are always found in pickling spice mixtures and often are part of spiced tea mixes. Allspice can also be purchased ground, ready to give a warm soothing flavor to cakes, fruit pies, fruit salads, hot fruit compotes, jams, vegetables, meats, poultry, fish, barbecue sauces, and soups. Allspice is the most popular spice used in Scandinavian cooking, where it is used in everything from pickled herring to bread. It really is an "allspice."

Basil or Sweet Basil

Basil comes from aromatic annual plants of the mint family. There are 50 to 60 varieties of basil including lemon basil, purple basil, cinnamon basil, and curly basil. Each has its own unique flavor and fragrance.

The most common variety is sweet basil, which has a complex peppery, licorice, and clove-like scent and flavor. It is the key ingredient in pesto. It has been called the tomato's best friend because it adds a wonderful flavor to both fresh tomato and cooked tomato dishes. Basil is also a great addition to salads and salad dressings, cheese sauces, egg dishes, pasta, fish, poultry, vegetables, soups, and stews. Basil makes even the most common dish a delectable treat.

Basil is available in fresh or dried form. Fresh basil is readily available in the summer but it must be handled with care as it bruises easily. Its volatile oil oxidizes and the basil will loose flavor when exposed to heat. It is best to add fresh basil at the very end of the cooking period to keep its sweet, rich flavor. Fresh basil can be used as whole leaves or it can be shredded, chopped, minced, or pureed. Dry basil is woody, rougher, and not as attractive as fresh basil. Dry basil should be finely crumbled with stems removed. Dry basil has a stronger flavor that has been described as a lemon and anise combination.

Chile Peppers

There are hundreds of varieties of chile peppers with a wide range of flavors and heat. You can't tell by appearance alone which pepper will be mild, hot, or super hot. Usually, the smaller the pepper, the hotter the pepper, but individual peppers will vary depending on growing conditions. There are also sections of the pepper that are hot spots. The heat comes from the capsaicin, which is concentrated at the stem end and is distributed along the white ribs and seeds inside the pepper. The heat can be mildly pleasant or dangerously hot. Heat rating scales have been developed and are sometimes indicated on the label of products made from chile peppers.

Chiles have been cultivated and used as part of the diet for at least 9,000 years. Christopher Columbus is credited with finding this fiery plant in the West Indies and bringing it back to Europe. The people in Europe believed the flavor resembled black pepper so they called it chile pepper.

Over the centuries, chiles have been used in foods and for medicinal purposes. Chiles were believed to have special healing qualities to help the liver, to aid digestion, to help urine production, to ease muscle pain, and to treat sore throats and toothaches. Chiles certainly do stimulate or irritate mucous membranes, so they probably do help loosen nasal and sinus congestion. Because chiles impart such a hot taste, it is a wonder that people in hot climates, such as Mexico, love their chiles. What really happens is that the hot chiles in food make the body sweat; as the perspiration evaporates, the body is cooled.

There is a large family of peppers that include chile peppers, bell peppers, and paprika peppers. Peppers of all varieties are rich in vitamins and minerals. All unripened peppers are green, but as they ripen some turn red, yellow, orange, or purple. Fresh peppers contain large amounts of vitamin C, and the rich color is an indication of the presence of vitamin A and phytochemicals.

Chiles are used in foods in various forms: fresh, dried, crushed, mashed, or juiced. Fresh peppers are great when you can get them, but care must be taken in handling hot chiles. When cutting or cooking with chiles, you may want to wear gloves. Avoid touching your eyes or other tender areas of your body when you handle the hot varieties. The capsaicin is oil soluble so washing your hands with plain water does not remove the heat.

Some of the common varieties and forms of chiles include:

Ancho Chile Peppers. These are large, dried, dark purple pods. They are the most common peppers used in Mexican cooking. The dried pods are soaked and then can be chopped and added to sauces, stews, beans, or rice.

Arbol Chile Peppers. Arbol peppers are bright red, thin, and graceful in appearance. They are about as hot as cayenne pepper.

Cayenne Red Pepper Powder. This powder is made from a blend of several small, ripe chiles. This pepper is made to be hot but in small amounts it gives a subtle great flavor that is especially helpful in low-fat or low-salt dishes.

Chile Flakes. A variety of chiles are chosen and then dried and crushed to form a blend of hot flavors. Chile flakes are often sprinkled on pizza and pasta. It is the pepper of choice in cooking when you want to see pieces of peppers in the dish and get a hot kick.

Chili Powder. This is an American blend of several spices. There are hundreds of blends but most contain varying amounts of ground chile peppers, cumin, and oregano. Some "secret" blends contain other herbs and spices. Chili powder is not particularly hot but it has a traditional robust flavor.

Chipotle Peppers. The chipotle chile is a jalapeño that has been smoked and dried. The chipotle adds a rich, smoky, hot flavor to food. It is used in traditional Southwest cooking. A dash of chipotle warms up everything from barbecue, stews, and soups, to beans, rice, breads, and salsa. Chipotle peppers in the powdered form can be served in a shaker to top tacos, sandwiches, meats, vegetables, casseroles, or salads.

Jalapeño Peppers. These are hot, but the heat is different from the cayenne pepper. The heat leaves your mouth faster and it is sensitive to cooking temperatures. For the best flavor, jalapeños should be added toward the end of cooking.

Paprika. This well-known spice is the powder of a particular mild chile pepper that gives food a sweet, mild, and lightly pungent taste and a reddish orange color. It is essential in many Hungarian, Spanish, and Balkan dishes.

Poblano Chile. This chile is commonly stuffed with cheese and then baked or fried. It is not eaten raw. The dried form is known as the ancho chile.

Tabasco Sauce. This is a special sauce made by combining hot red chiles with vinegar.

Tien Tsin Chile Peppers. These are tiny and very hot. They are often added whole to Asian dishes such as soups and stir-fries. Pick them out if you do not want to burn your mouth.

Some other varieties of chile peppers include serrano, pasilla, guajillo, cascabel, sanaam, piquin, dundicut, seco, morron, guindilla, lombok, and habanero.

If you make a mistake and eat a dish that is too hot for your taste, drink a glass of milk, or eat some yogurt or ice cream quickly. Drinking plain water will not work because the capsaicin is oil based and water will not put the fire out. Beer is a second choice because the alcohol helps to dissolve the oils.

How to Roast Fresh Chiles and Other Peppers

Roasting chiles gives them a special flavor that you cannot get with any other method of pepper preparation. It involves removing the tough outer skin of the pepper by roasting over an open flame, in a hot barbecue grill, or under a broiler.

(Remember to wear plastic gloves and never touch your face, eyes, or other tender parts of your body while working with chiles.)

Place the chiles or peppers on a lightly oiled baking sheet under a very hot broiler. Place the peppers about 3 to 6 inches from the heating unit or flames. Watch carefully and turn the pods frequently for even blistering. The skin should turn black and blister. Any area that does not blacken and blister will not peel.

When pepper skins have blistered, place peppers in a closed paper bag for 5 to 10 minutes to allow the steam to soften the skin.

Remove peppers from the bag and peel off the skin. Discard skin. Slice peppers and store in the refrigerator.

Cilantro

Cilantro is the leaf and coriander is the seed of the same plant. However the plant can give us only one of the two. If the leaves are harvested, then the seed is not produced. If the seed is allowed to grow and mature, the leaves are too old and bitter to use in cooking. Thus you may get two great taste sensations from one plant, but if you're growing just one plant, you must choose between the two.

Cilantro comes from the small parsley-like leaves of the plant, which have a distinct pungent flavor. It takes some people several tries before they really appreciate its taste. It is commonly sold in large food markets but sometime it is labeled "fresh coriander" or "Chinese parsley" instead of "cilantro." Fresh cilantro is highly perishable. It will last for about a week in the refrigerator.

Cilantro leaves are essential in some Mexican dishes. They are used in picante sauces, salsas, soups, rice dishes, bean dishes, chicken and fish dishes, fruit desserts, and chutneys. It is best to add cilantro at the end of cooking to unleash the musty, nutty flavor.

Cinnamon

There is an aura of warmth and a taste of homemade with cinnamon. Cinnamon, as we know it in the United States, is from the beautiful cassia evergreen tree. It is actually the inner bark, which is ground into a powder. Cinnamon sticks come from thinly sliced bark from the upper branches. They are left to dry, which allows the bark to curl. Cinnamon sticks have less flavor than ground cinnamon, which comes from older bark that is stronger and more flavorful. The cinnamon stick, however, is a pleasing addition to coffee and specialty drinks.

The world's first form of cinnamon and the preferred form of cinnamon in England and Mexico comes from the island of Ceylon. Ceylon has been known as the cinnamon capital of the world since biblical times. When the Dutch ruled in the 1600s, cinnamon was valued so highly that the penalty for the illegal sale of even a single stick of cinnamon was death. Cinnamon from Ceylon has a unique citrus flavor and the color is lighter than cassia.

Most of the cassia cinnamon we use in the United States comes from Asian countries. Korintje cassia cinnamon comes from Mount Kerinci, which gives this cinnamon its name. It is sweet and mellow and often used in those famous commercial cinnamon buns. The cassia from Vietnam has a high oil content and has the strongest cinnamon flavor. It was a favorite of American chefs but it has not been readily available since the war in

Vietnam. The cassia cinnamon from China is generally considered the best overall cinnamon. Its familiar sweet cassia cinnamon taste suits the tastes of most Americans.

Cumin

Cumin is a spice that has been used for thousands of years. It has been found in the tombs of the Egyptians, it is mentioned in the Bible, Hippocrates used it for medicinal purposes, and the Romans used it as a substitute for pepper. Today cumin seed is used whole and ground in cooking a wide variety of foods. Cumin is best known as the essential spice in curry powder blends and chili powder.

The earthy, pungent flavor of cumin has been rediscovered in the United States due to the growing interest in ethnic foods. The spice flavors foods of the Middle East, North Africa, India, Spain, Germany, Mexico, Latin America, and the American Southwest.

Cumin is an aromatic spice that has a strong, warm, slightly bitter taste. A little bit goes a long way. Try using only 1/16 to 1/4 teaspoon in recipes that serve four. Just a pinch of cumin adds zest to simple dishes and sauces. Cumin will enhance the flavor of chili, curry dishes, oriental stir-fry dishes, soups, stews, ground meat mixtures, cheese casseroles, pasta and rice dishes, and vegetables.

Curry Powder

What is curry powder? Does it come from a seed, a root, or a leaf? Actually it is all of the above. Curry is not a single spice. Curry powder is a blend of many spices, and there are as many curry mixtures as there are Indian cooks. Curry powder can be a mixture of 6 to 20 different spices that are roasted and ground together. The common spices used include: coriander, turmeric, fenugreek, garlic, ginger, sweet paprika, cayenne pepper, white pepper, cumin, nutmeg, fennel, cinnamon, cardamom, allspice, mustard seeds, saffron, black pepper, and chile peppers.

Cooking with curry is cooking with creativity. Indian cooks prepare unique spice blends for different dishes. There are sweet curries for vegetable or fruit dishes and hot pungent curries for heavier meat dishes. A curry in India is any cooked dish that uses a variety of spices. A traditional curry meal will be a curry sauce combined with meat and rice. This will be served with a variety of relishes and garnishes that are passed to the guests. The side dishes may include mango or other fruit chutney, peanuts, coconut, raisins, peppers, or fresh fruits.

A curried dish will never have the same taste and it will challenge the taste buds. There is an Indian belief that eating more complex and subtly flavored foods exercises the brain, making it more capable of understanding and appreciating the subtle complexities of life. For novice taste buds, heavy curry dishes may seem a bit overwhelming. The key is to start by adding very small amounts of curry powder to foods you already know and like. Try a variety of curry powders and sprinkle on poultry, fish, or meat before baking; add to egg dishes; add to sandwich spreads; blend with cream cheese, soft cheese or grated cheese for canapés; add to basic white sauces; or add to vegetable and lentil soups. Just a pinch of curry will provide a mysterious, tantalizing flavor to common dishes.

True Indian cooks will create their own curry mixtures from whole spices, which they heat and grind to give a lightly toasted flavor. In the United States, a variety of curry powder blends are available at specialty spice stores. The mixtures will range from sweet to varying degrees of hotness. There are some curries that are very traditional regional blends. There is a Balti Seasoning influenced by the Baltistan region in northern Pakistan. The Rogan Josh Seasoning is a spicy mixture used to cover up the strong taste of lamb or mutton in northern India and Pakistan. Vindaloo Seasoning is a hot and spicy blend that comes from Goa, a small state in the middle of the Malabar coast of India.

Use the traditions of centuries to bring new flavors into your kitchen and spice up your life.

Dill Weed

Dill weed has been important in cooking since the Middle Ages and it is still one of the most popular seasonings used today in American cooking. The plant produces feathery leaves and yellowish-brown dill seeds. The dill weed is lighter and sweeter than the seed. It is world famous as an ingredient in the canning of dill pickles.

Dill weed has a wondrous bouquet when used sparingly. It perks up yogurt, sour cream, and cheese sauces. A touch of dill weed is fantastic sprinkled on omelets, salads, soups, and breads.

Garlic

Garlic is the most heavily used flavoring in the world. It has been affectionately called the "stinking rose" because of it pungent aroma and flavor. It contains an array of naturally-occurring flavorful compounds.

Garlic has been touted for its medicinal powers for thousands of years. There are claims that garlic reduces blood cholesterol levels, reduces the risk of blood clots, reduces blood pressure, reduces

cancer risk, has antibiotic qualities, fights infections, and aids digestion. Hundreds of scientific studies have searched the real health benefits of this unique plant. While we can't be sure of its life-sustaining properties, we do know that it pleases the palate.

The garlic bulb is made up of many small cloves that hold the secret compounds. Allicin is considered the active ingredient in garlic. It is best to crush the clove of garlic with the flat side of a chef's knife and then mince it by hand to release the allicin. To cook garlic, use a small amount of oil and cook over low heat. Never let garlic burn, since it turns sharp and acrid when browned on high heat. If you prefer a milder taste, leave the cloves whole while simmering in soups, stocks, or vegetables.

Baked garlic is surprisingly sweet and the cloves become soft and spreadable. To bake garlic, remove some of the outer husks, leaving a thin layer of peel. Slice off the tapered end of the garlic head. Place in a small ovenproof dish. Drizzle with a small amount of olive oil. Cover and bake at 350 degrees for 45 minutes. Uncover and bake another 45 minutes until cloves are soft. The baked cloves make a great substitute for high-fat spreads such as butter or margarine.

Garlic powder is dehydrated ground garlic. It is easy to use in recipes or to sprinkle directly on meats, vegetables, and breads. The usual amount to use is 1/4 teaspoon garlic powder to replace 1 clove of garlic. In some dishes, however, there is no good substitute for fresh garlic.

Store fresh garlic bulbs in a cool, dry, airy place. Bulbs will rot if closed in a plastic bag. They are best stored in a covered terra-cotta jar with holes in the sides. Garlic stored in this way can last for months.

Include cooked or raw garlic frequently in your meals for that pungent, fresh taste, and you may even receive a health benefit, too.

Ginger

When you pick up a piece of ginger, you may wonder how something so strange looking, almost grotesque looking, can taste so good. It is one of those times when you have to look more than skin deep to find beauty. Ginger grows under the ground as a special type of stem called a rhizome, but most people identify it as a root. The inside of this unattractive root gives us the wonderful warm tastes and aromas of ginger.

Ginger is grown commercially in India, China, Africa, and Jamaica. Ginger can be purchased as a whole fresh root or dried root. Ginger can also be cut into pieces and pickled or preserved in syrup. A real sweet treat is crystallized ginger, which is small pieces of ginger that are dried and rolled in sugar. The most common form of ginger used in most kitchens is powdered ginger.

Some people believe ginger has special health-giving properties. It is believed to improve digestion and warm the stomach. It may even be helpful in relieving the feeling of nausea and travel sickness. Ginger also adds spark and interest to life. A lively person is described as "full of ginger."

Ginger as a spice is used with meat and poultry, especially in stir-fry meals. Ginger is wonderful in soups, salads, vegetables, fruits, and desserts. Ginger is often combined with cinnamon and nutmeg.

Mustard

Mustard is one of the oldest culinary and medicinal spices. The oldest known recipe for mustard was written in the 1st century AD. The mustard seeds are the fruit of the mustard plant. They are used for pickling and sausage making, and the smaller brown seeds, which are hotter, are used in traditional Asian, Indian, and African cooking.

Dry mustard comes from whole mustard seeds that are crushed, ground, and sifted. The powder is very fine and resembles flour. The flavor of mustard is locked in the powder and is only released when cool water is added. The flavor is produced by enzyme reactions that are activated by cool water. When a recipe calls for dry mustard, it is best to mix the dry mustard with a small amount of water to form a paste, let it sit for about 10 minutes, and then add the paste to your dish. Boiling water destroys the enzymes and the full flavor will not develop. After adding water, other liquids such as vinegar, wine, and beer can be added.

The mustard seed is a spice, but when it is ground and prepared with water and other seasonings, it becomes a condiment. Mustard is one of the most popular condiments in the United States. Mustard seed, mustard powder, and prepared mustards are used in sauces, salad dressings, vegetables, and meat, fish, poultry, and bean dishes.

There are hundreds of recipes for prepared mustards. The Mustard Museum, in Mount Horeb, Wisconsin, devoted only to mustards sells over 500 different kinds. For a standard mustard, use 8 parts mustard powder to 7 parts liquid. A base recipe follows:

> 1 cup mustard powder
> 1/3 cup cool water

1/3 cup vinegar
1/2 teaspoon salt
1 tablespoon honey

Mix mustard powder and cool water together to form a smooth paste. Let sit about 10 minutes. Add remaining ingredients. Add any herb or seasoning of your choice. Pack in airtight jar. Store in refrigerator.

Nutmeg and Mace

Nutmeg and mace grow together as sister and brother. They are the product of 40 to 70 foot statuesque nutmeg trees. The tree originated and still grows in Indonesia, but the tiny Caribbean island of Grenada is known for the best nutmeg in the world. The nutmeg tree produces a yellow fruit that resembles an apricot or peach. When it ripens it splits open to reveal its secret treasures. There is a brilliant red lacy covering over a hard oval-shaped shell. The lacy covering outside the shell is the mace and the seed inside the shell is the nutmeg. The mace and the nutmeg are both dried.

Mace suffers from a poor public image because of its name. Mace is the name of a spiked club that was used in the Middle Ages for breaking armor. It is also the brand name of a defensive pepper spray. The mace spice has no relationship to the Mace pepper spray. In fact, the mace spice has a sweet, refined taste and may even remind you of being in a bakery. It is a traditional flavoring used in doughnuts, pastries, fruit cakes, muffins, and pumpkin pie. The more adventuresome cook will use mace in soups and in barbecue sauce for grilled meat and fish. Mace is usually sold ground because it has a low oil content, thus its flavor is stable.

Nutmeg is wonderful but the flavor can be easily lost. Because nutmeg has a high oil content, it should be grated when you are ready to use it. The flavor is so superior that the few extra seconds of grating it yourself will be well worth your effort. Nutmeg can be used in both sweet and savory dishes. It is common in desserts and breads. It is wonderful in potato and vegetable dishes, white pasta sauces, and in most egg and cheese dishes.

Oregano

Oregano is the Italian and Spanish name for wild marjoram. It resembles marjoram in flavor but oregano is stronger. There are many different varieties ranging from mild to strong. The mild-flavored oregano is grown in cool climates and the strong-flavored oregano is grown in hot, dry climates.

Oregano has been indispensable to Italian, Greek, and Mexican cooking through the ages. It is known as the classic pizza and pasta seasoning. It has a bold aroma and a hot, biting taste and is an essential in chili powder blends. When used in simmered tomato sauces and other foods requiring long slow cooking, it holds its flavor. It also keeps it flavor well when dried. The amount of oregano to add to a dish is a matter of taste. Italian cooks may use two to three times as much in a dish as French cooks.

Paprika

Paprika is an indispensable spice that garnishes and dresses up foods with rich color and subtle flavor. Paprika comes from peppers that grow on certain capsicum plants that look like tomato plants. The peppers are ground to produce a powder that is a rich, dark red color with a mild, sweet flavor, a hint of heat, and a pleasant aroma. The peppers are imported from Spain, Hungary, and Yugoslavia, but they are also grown in California.

The peppers are ripened, dried, and ground. Although the peppers are high in vitamin C, much of it is destroyed in the heat processing. Peppers are also high in vitamin A and beta carotene, which are heat stable.

Pepper—Black and White

Pepper is the king of all spices. Although we take it for granted, at times in history pepper costed as much, ounce for ounce, as gold and silver. Today it is one of the least expensive, yet most desired spices. It grows as the fruit on a vine that is abundant in warm tropical forests. The best peppers are picked from the vine when the peppercorns are large and fully mature. For the best flavor, peppercorns must be handled and stored carefully.

Pepper can be green, black, or white. Peppers are green when picked but as they dry, they become the familiar black peppercorns we use every day. Drying is necessary to preserve them. Green peppers will spoil quickly unless they are preserved in some way, so they are either dried or pickled. (Pickled green peppers are called capers.) White pepper is actually the inside of the black peppercorns. Black pepper is soaked in water until the outer coating can be removed. The pale gray inside of the peppercorn is dried in the sun to whiten it.

There are also pink or red peppercorns. These are not really related to the black peppercorns but they are the same size and shape. The attractive bright color adds interest and a rich, sweet, peppery flavor to foods.

Pepper is the perfect and most essential seasoning for a variety of foods. The choice of black or white pepper is a matter of personal taste. White pepper has a unique taste and provides a hot bite to foods. It is the best choice to use in light-colored foods such as white sauces and potatoes.

The best pepper is the freshest pepper, therefore, a good pepper grinder is essential in every kitchen and on every table. The discerning palate tastes a vast difference between the ground pepper from the pepper shaker versus the freshly ground pepper from your own pepper mill.

Pepper—Cayenne

Cayenne pepper is made from a combination of hot red peppers from the family of capsicum plants, commonly called red peppers or chiles. The peppers are dried and ground to produce a seasoning with a specific heat index. The ground spice is about 100 times hotter than the familiar jalapeño pepper.

Cayenne pepper is the most pungent of all spices. It adds an indispensable flavor to many dishes, including meats, vegetables, casseroles, sauces, salad dressings, cream cheese dishes, etc. Since the ground cayenne pepper is always hot, be careful when adding to foods. You can always add more after tasting. A small bit adds a touch of intrigue and wonderful flavor to a variety of food, but too much can be painful.

Tarragon

Tarragon is a hardy perennial plant native to Russia, but the herb is especially popular in French cooking. It combines beautifully with wine- and shallot-based dishes.

Tarragon is growing in popularity in the United States because it can add a key flavoring to everyday foods. Tarragon is used in meat, poultry, seafood, egg, and vegetable dishes. It adds sweetness to many sauces such as bearnaise, tartar, herb butter, mayonnaise, and mustards. Tarragon vinegar is a popular ingredient in dressings.

Tarragon has an unusual, sweet anise-like flavor and a licorice fragrance. It is mild, yet it can be powerful and overwhelming if used in large amounts. The best advice for using tarragon is to use it sparingly. Use less, not more when in doubt. Fresh tarragon has the best flavor and it is available all summer and fall.

Thyme

Thyme is a perennial plant of the mint family that is native to the Mediterranean region where it grows wild. Hundreds of varieties are now cultivated in the United States and many other countries.

Thyme has a complex, vibrant flavor that has been described as peppery with a pine tree aroma. It is essential in Southern cooking and is especially good with poultry and pork. It also provides a special flavor to meat, fish, shellfish, soups, stews, stocks, stuffings, bean dishes, and marinades. It is a must for pea soup with ham. Dried thyme has the same good flavor as fresh thyme, but the flavor oxidizes and almost disappears when exposed to heat. For the best flavor, it is best to add thyme toward the end of the cooking time.

Vanilla

What would life be like without vanilla? There is no substitute for the rich, smooth flavor of vanilla in custards, sauces, and desserts. The very best vanilla is real vanilla, which is a complex mixture of hundreds of flavor components. The real extract is made by percolating vanilla beans in an alcohol and water solution, much like you make coffee. The major fla-

vor component of vanilla comes from vanillin. The chemical structure of vanillin has been identified and it can be reproduced in a chemistry laboratory. Vanillin is used to make artificial vanilla but because there are many other flavor components of the vanilla bean that are left behind, it can never come close to matching the wonderful, robust flavor of pure vanilla extract.

Vanilla comes from an orchid plant that grows well in Madagascar, Mexico, and some parts of Central America. The plant produces a lovely flower that is unique in that it cannot fertilize itself. There is a tough membrane that separates the stamen from the pistil and thus it must be hand pollinated. Once pollinated, the plant produces a thin green pod about 6 to 10 inches long. It is harvested while still green and then cured over several months. The beans are warmed in the sun and placed in "sweat" boxes where fermentation occurs. The pods become wrinkled and brown as the chemical vanillin develops. They are then ready to be chopped and percolated with alcohol and warm water. The liquid is strained, aged, and preserved in dark bottles. Vanilla is made either double strength or single strength. The double strength vanilla is made by using twice as many beans (about 200 beans) to make each gallon of extract. This special concentrated vanilla has been the secret ingredient of professional bakers for years.

Whole vanilla beans can be used in making some desserts. For desserts that are cooked on top of the stove in a liquid base, cut the bean in half, split it lengthwise with a knife, and add it to the liquid. The bean should remain in the liquid during the cooking process. For baked desserts, substitute vanilla sugar for the plain sugar in the recipe. Vanilla sugar is prepared by storing whole vanilla beans in the sugar canister. The beans should be buried in the sugar and the canister tightly closed. As you use the sugar, add more sugar to keep the beans completely covered. The vanilla sugar can be used in recipes that would be enhanced with a rich sweetness.

10 More Optional Spices

Bay Leaves

Bay leaves come from a beautiful small evergreen tree that has been cultivated since antiquity in Mediterranean countries. The aromatic, smooth, waxy leaves are 1 to 3 inches long. They have a spicy aroma and a mild, pleasantly bitter flavor. Bay leaves are indispensable in Mediterranean dishes such as soups, stews, meat and game dishes, stocks, sauces, marinades, and vegetables.

Bay leaves are usually used whole but are also available ground. When whole, they must be simmered in liquid to release their volatile oils, which provide the flavor. Use one or two leaves in a medium-size pot of stock, soup, or sauce. The longer they are steeped in liquid, the more pronounced the flavor becomes. Remember to remove the bay leaves before serving the dish. When using ground bay leaves, the aroma is released quickly and flavor can be lost if cooked for a long time. Ground bay leaves are best used in sautéed and grilled foods.

Cardamom

Cardamom is one of the most valued spices in the world, but it is certainly not one of the most common in the United States. Many people cook for a lifetime without ever using cardamom. In Scandinavia it is used in cakes, cookies, and breads, and it is the secret ingredient in Swedish meatballs. In India it is an important ingredient in meat and vegetable dishes. People in the Arab world use cardamom (often in large amounts) to flavor coffee for special occasions.

Cardamom comes from the small green fruit of a tall tropical plant. The fruit looks like a pod the size of a lima bean, but it has three flat sides. The pod must be harvested by hand from the plant stalks. Inside the pod are 10 to 20 small seeds, which are the cardamom spice we use in cooking. The pods protect the seeds during storage but have little flavor. The pods can be fairly easily opened by crushing with your fingers, rolling with a rolling pin, or smashing with a mortar and pestle. Discard the pods and crush the seeds. The pods are usually green but some pods are bleached white. There is also a black cardamom that is used in African cooking. It has a unique strong smoky flavor.

Cardamom can be purchased in three ways: (1) whole pods, (2) whole seeds removed from the pods, and (3) ground seeds. The ground seeds are the most convenient but professional cooks believe the whole seeds, that you crush or grind yourself, have the best flavor. In the spice business, there is always the chance that the ground spice can be adulterated with an inexpensive filler.

In ancient Rome, cardamom was used to make perfume and may still be used for some perfumes today. Cardamom is often part of the fragrant sachet bags used in closets and clothes drawers. Another ancient practice that is still common today in Europe is chewing cardamom seeds to take away bad breath. Cardamom is also thought to be an aphrodisiac. (Maybe there is a connection with the sweeter breath.) The Arabs in ancient times described this special spice as the "grain of paradise."

Cloves

Cloves are the unopened flower bud from a magnificent evergreen tree. It is native to certain islands in the East Indies that are known as the Spice Islands. There is a long history revolving around the control of the world market for cloves. In the 1500s and 1600s, cloves were actually worth more than their weight in gold. The Dutch so strictly controlled the distribution of cloves that anyone who planted a clove tree without government permission was executed. The death

penalty for smuggling cloves was still a law in Africa as late as 1970.

Clove trees produce pink flower buds that are hand picked and sun dried. They shrivel and turn a reddish-brown color. Cloves complement ham, pork, sausage, and game. The buds can be added to tea, cider, and mulled wine. The dried clove buds can also be ground. In the powdered form, they are often an ingredient in fruit pies, cakes, cookies, sweet breads, baked fruits, chutney, and vegetables. Cloves are often used in combination with cinnamon, ginger, and nutmeg.

Cloves are considered a strong spice and can easily overwhelm a dish, giving it a hot bitter taste. Just one clove in a pot of stew can provide an intriguing, subtle taste. (Remember to remove it before serving to prevent someone from choking on the bud.)

Coriander

Coriander is related closely to the familiar herb cilantro (see page 16). Coriander is the seed and cilantro is the leaf of the same plant, which grows in warm climates around the world, from Africa to Europe to South America. It is even grown in the United States, especially in Kentucky. Coriander seeds have been found in Egyptian tombs and they are mentioned several times in the Old Testament of the Bible. The Greeks recommend it as a medicinal tonic, and in the Middle East people add a seed to coffee or tea to aid digestion. In the United States it is in a wide variety of products from hot dogs to gin to perfume.

The flavor of coriander can be described as a mixture of orange, anise, and cumin, or a mixture of lemon peel and sage. Coriander is a familiar spice in sweet biscuits, breads, cakes, cookies, pastries, and candy. It is that secret ingredient that some cooks believe makes pea soup so special. The coriander seed is one of the spices used in making pickles. Coriander complements poultry stuffings and is great when rubbed on pork or beef roasts. Coriander is also the major ingredient in curry powder and it is often used in other spice blends and condiments.

Crushed Red Pepper

A variety of chile peppers are dried and crushed to form a blend of hot flavors. Chile flakes are often sprinkled on pizza and pasta. It is the pepper of choice in cooking when you want to see pieces of peppers in the dish and get a hot kick.

Marjoram

Marjoram is a beautiful aromatic perennial plant when grown in warm climates and an annual plant when grown in cold climates. Greek legend held that it was the favorite herb of the goddess of love. It was believed that you would dream of your future spouse if you anointed yourself with marjoram before you went to bed. The fragrance is so pleasant that today marjoram is used in potpourri and sachets.

Marjoram has a flavor similar to oregano but it is more delicate and sweet. It can substitute for the strong flavor of sage in poultry dressing if you prefer a less pungent flavor. Marjoram complements thyme, basil, garlic, and onions. It is often used in commercial spice blends.

Marjoram is frequently found in Polish, Italian, Mexican, and French cooking. The Polish sausage called kielbasa uses marjoram as an essential ingredient. Marjoram is often an ingredient in recipes for fish, poultry, beef, vegetables, stews, soups, and salad dressings. It is best to add marjoram toward the end of cooking to avoid losing its flavor.

Parsley

Parsley has been cultivated for at least 2,000 years and it still one of the most used herbs throughout the world. There are more than 30 varieties. Some have curly leaves and others have flat leaves. It is a rich source of both vitamin A and vitamin C and it is popular as a breath freshener for garlic lovers.

Parsley is used both for garnishing and for flavoring foods. In the fresh form it adds color and interest to plates of food. Parsley brings out the flavor of other spices and herbs and it seems to reduce the need for salt in soups and sauces. Chopped parsley can be added to almost any food, including meat, fish, poultry, and cheese and egg dishes to add color and a bittersweet pungent flavor. Dried parsley is not as good as fresh but it can be used in a pinch.

Rosemary

Rosemary comes from a bushy evergreen shrub of the mint family. It has pine needle-like leaves with a bittersweet flavor. The oils extracted from the flowers and the foliage produce a beautiful fragrance used in perfumes.

Rosemary has a piney aroma and a minty sweetness. It is often paired with oregano and thyme in Italian dishes. Rosemary is good in marinades, cream soups, stews, meat, and poultry dishes. It adds a special taste and flavor to jams, fruit salsas, vinegar, and herb butters. Fresh rosemary makes an attractive garnish for summer drinks and fruit salads.

Rosemary is good both fresh and dried but it should be used in small amounts. Dried rosemary is usually best if it is crushed before adding it to your recipe. Large amounts will overpower a dish—just a pinch will do.

Saffron

Saffron is the true spice of intrigue and mystery. It might also be a little intimidating to use since it is the most expensive spice in the world. Why should 1 gram (the weight of one paper clip) cost around $10? Because one gram is made up of 450 tiny threads and each thread is a stigma that is found in the middle of the flower of the saffron crocus. This crocus plant is only 12 inches tall and the flowers have to be picked by hand. There are one to three stigmas in each flower and each must be picked out by hand and carefully dried. It takes 75,000 flowers to make 1 pound of saffron.

The good news is that it takes very small amounts of saffron to create a fragrant, flavorful meal. Each orange-colored stigma dries to a deep burgundy color. The stigma is then called a thread. A small pinch of saffron equals about 20 threads, a medium pinch 35 threads, and a large pinch 50 threads. A small pinch of saffron will cost about 50 cents, and that will be enough to give a light golden yellow color and a prized saffron flavor to saffron rice that serves four or several quarts of chicken soup.

It is best to buy saffron in the form of threads that you can identify as real saffron. The powdered form can be adulterated easily. It is common to find "bargain saffron" in the powdered form when really it has been diluted with turmeric or other inexpensive flower petals. Cheating with saffron has been going on since the Middle Ages but at that time in Europe, the penalty for selling adulterated saffron was death. Burning at the stake was the sentence.

The crocus that gives us the most wonderful saffron grows in Kashmir in northern India but it is not always available. Spanish saffron is also very good and it is the most common source of saffron sold in the United States.

Since very small amounts of saffron are used in each recipe it is important to get it distributed evenly during the cooking process. Count out the threads that will be used and soak them for 10 to 15 minutes in a small amount of the liquid that will be used in the recipe. The dried threads will expand and release their color and flavor into the liquid. Add both the threads and liquid to the recipe. The saffron can also be pulverized with a mortar and pestle and added to the dry ingredients of a recipe.

There are other spices, such as turmeric, that will give a yellow color to your dish, but there is no spice that can substitute for the distinctive flavor of saffron. Saffron is a spice of beauty and marvelous taste.

Turmeric

Turmeric is an unforgettable spice once you have seen it. It imparts a deep yellow color to everything it touches. Ground turmeric is a brilliant orange-yellow color that has been used for centuries in dyes, perfumes, and cosmetics, and as a flavoring in foods. Before the development of commercial dyes, turmeric was used to dye fabrics. In some cultures, it was used to color the skin to produce a healthy golden glow. Marco Polo is credited with introducing turmeric to Europe as a substitute for the very expensive saffron. Turmeric may give food a similar color as saffron, but the flavor is not the same.

The ground turmeric used in cooking comes from the root (actually the rhizomes) of the tropical turmeric plant. The rhizomes are fat stems that run underground and are similar in size to the ginger root. The fresh or dried root can be purchased in specialty stores but turmeric is usually sold in powdered form.

Turmeric imparts a warm, sweet flavor to food. It complements other spices and is commonly used in spice blends. Turmeric is the most essential ingredient in curry powder. Curry powder would not be yellow without turmeric. Many condiments and prepared mustards also use turmeric for richness of color and flavor. It is used commercially in salad dressings, pickles, relishes, margarine, and cheese to enhance their color.

Appetizers

Artichoke, Mushroom, and Red Pepper Pizza

 Italian seasonings add just the right flavor to this colorful, healthy pizza. Serve it for supper or cut it in small pieces for a special appetizer.

10 ounces pizza dough

1 tablespoon olive oil

1 medium red bell pepper, thinly sliced

1/2 pound fresh mushrooms

3 cloves garlic, minced

1 teaspoon basil

1/2 teaspoon oregano

1/4 teaspoon rosemary, crushed

14 ounces artichoke hearts, frozen or canned

1/2 pound grated mozzarella cheese

crushed red pepper flakes, optional

Preheat oven to 425°. Lightly grease a 14 x 10 inch nonstick baking pan. Unroll pizza dough and pat evenly into the pan. Bake for 5 minutes. Remove from oven and set aside. In a medium skillet, heat oil. Over medium heat, cook peppers and mushrooms until tender. Add garlic, basil, oregano, and rosemary. Cook 1 minute. Add artichokes and stir gently to mix. Remove from heat. Drain off any liquid. Sprinkle half of cheese over prepared crust. Spread vegetable mixture evenly over cheese. Top with remaining cheese. Bake for 10 minutes or until crust is lightly browned and cheese is melted. Top with crushed red pepper flakes if desired.

Serves 4

Nutrition Information per serving:
Calories: 400 – Fat: 15 gm. – Protein: 24 gm.
Carbohydrate: 44 gm. – Cholesterol: 30 mg. – Fiber: high

Baked Brie Stuffed with Smoked Salmon

 The combination of smoked salmon with fresh herbs tucked inside warm Brie cheese makes this a memorable party appetizer.

8 ounce round of Brie cheese, well chilled

1/2 cup fresh basil, minced

1/4 teaspoon oregano

1/4 teaspoon thyme

1/4 teaspoon rosemary

2 ounces smoked salmon or thinly sliced lox

2 tablespoons balsamic vinegar

1 tablespoon honey

Remove rind from the sides and top of the Brie cheese. With a sharp serrated knife, slice the cheese into three pieces horizontally. Place the cheese piece with the rind in a pie plate. (Place rind side down.) In a small bowl, combine basil, oregano, thyme, and rosemary. Press a third of the seasonings on the cheese round and cover with half of the smoked salmon. Lay another cheese round on top and press another third of the seasoning on top, followed by the other half of the salmon. Lay the last layer of cheese on top. Press the last third of the seasoning on top. Chill for at least 1 hour or it can be covered and stored in the refrigerator for a day before baking.

When ready to bake, preheat oven to 450°. Bake for 8 to 12 minutes or until cheese begins to melt. Mix vinegar and honey together and pour over cheese. Serve with crackers or small pieces of French bread.

Serves 8

Nutrition Information per serving without the crackers:
Calories: 110 – Fat: 8 gm. – Protein: 7 gm.
Carbohydrate: 3 gm. – Cholesterol: 30 mg. – Fiber: low

Black Bean Spread

 Choose any variety of canned beans but be sure to use fresh cilantro. Make it as hot as you like it with cayenne pepper.

15-ounce can black beans, drained

1/2 cup salsa, hot or mild

2 tablespoons lime juice

2 tablespoons fresh cilantro

1/4 teaspoon cumin powder

1/2 teaspoon sugar

salt to taste

cayenne pepper to taste

cilantro for garnish

Combine beans, salsa, lime juice, cilantro, cumin, and sugar in a food processor. Process until smooth. Adjust seasoning with salt and pepper to taste. Garnish with additional chopped cilantro. Spread on crackers or warm tortilla wedges.

Serves 8

Nutrition Information per serving:
Calories: 55 – Fat: 1 gm. – Protein: 3 gm.
Carbohydrate: 9 – Cholesterol: 0 mg. – Fiber: high

Broccoli, Ham, and Cheese Strata

 This strata could be served in small pieces as an appetizer or in larger portions for a breakfast or lunch meal. It has lots of flavor with the dry mustard, basil, and rosemary. Add extra pepper if you like it hotter.

1 tablespoon butter or margarine	6 eggs, lightly beaten
1 medium onion, finely chopped	1 teaspoon Worcestershire sauce
1/2 medium red pepper, finely chopped	2 teaspoons dry mustard
10 ounces fresh or frozen broccoli, chopped	1 teaspoon basil
8 slices lightly toasted bread	1/2 teaspoon rosemary, crushed
12 ounces (3 cups) grated low-fat cheddar cheese	1/2 teaspoon pepper
	1 teaspoon salt
1/2 pound lean ham, diced	2 1/2 cups fat-free milk

Grease a 9 x 13 inch baking pan. Heat butter in medium skillet. Add onion and cook over medium heat until translucent. Add red pepper, broccoli, and 2 tablespoons water. Cover and cook until vegetables are tender. Set aside. Cut bread into 1-inch cubes and spread in bottom of pan. Spoon vegetables evenly over the bread. Sprinkle with half of the cheese. Top with ham. In a large bowl combine eggs, Worcestershire sauce, dry mustard, basil, rosemary, pepper, salt, and milk. Beat until well mixed. Pour into baking pan. Sprinkle with remaining cheese. Press down lightly to make sure bread can soak up the egg mixture. Cover and refrigerate several hours or overnight. It can be refrigerated for several days before baking.

When ready to bake, preheat oven to 325°. Bake uncovered for 1 hour or until lightly browned and knife inserted in the middle comes out clean. Let stand 10 minutes before cutting.

Note: To make one 8 x 8 inch pan, prepare half the recipe.

Serves 10

Nutrition Information per serving:
Calories: 235 – Fat: 9 gm. – Protein: 21 gm.
Carbohydrate: 17 gm. – Cholesterol: 130 mg. – Fiber: medium

Curry Olive Cheese Spread on English Muffins

The hint of curry adds a tantalizing flavor to this easy hot lunch sandwich.
To serve as an appetizer cut each English muffin into bite-size pieces.

1 cup black olives, chopped

6 green onions, chopped

2 cups grated low-fat cheddar cheese

1/2 cup fat-free mayonnaise

1/2 teaspoon hot curry powder

1/4 teaspoon garlic powder

3 English muffins

In a medium bowl, combine olives, onions, cheese, mayonnaise, curry powder, and garlic powder. Mix well with a spoon. Store in covered bowl and refrigerate until ready to serve.

Preheat oven broiler when ready to serve. Spread cheese mixture 1/2-inch thick on English muffin halves. Place on baking pan. Broil until bubbly and lightly browned. Watch carefully to prevent burning.

Serves 6

Nutrition Information per serving:
Calories: 225 – Fat: 6 gm. – Protein: 14 gm.
Carbohydrate: 29 gm. – Cholesterol: 19 mg. – Fiber: medium

Easy Garden Bake

 The Italian seasonings complement the mild fresh vegetables. This is so easy and healthy too.

1 cup zucchini, thinly sliced	2 eggs, lightly beaten
1 large fresh tomato, seeded and chopped	1/4 teaspoon thyme
1 medium onion, finely chopped	1/4 teaspoon oregano
1 medium red bell pepper, finely chopped	1/4 teaspoon marjoram
1 medium green pepper, finely chopped	1/4 teaspoon basil
1 cup grated low-fat Swiss cheese	1/4 teaspoon white pepper
3/4 cup fat-free milk	1/2 teaspoon salt
2/3 cup reduced-fat baking mix	1/2 cup freshly grated Parmesan cheese

Preheat oven to 400°. Butter a 10-inch glass pie pan. Arrange zucchini, tomatoes, onions, and peppers in pan. Sprinkle with Swiss cheese. In a small bowl, combine milk, baking mix, eggs, thyme, oregano, marjoram, basil, white pepper, and salt. Mix well with electric mixer until smooth. Pour in the pan over vegetables. Sprinkle with Parmesan cheese. Bake for 35 to 45 minutes or until knife inserted in center comes out clean. Turn oven to 350° if it is browning too quickly. Cool 10 minutes before cutting.

Serves 6

Nutrition Information per serving:
Calories: 190 – Fat: 6 gm. – Protein: 14 gm.
Carbohydrate: 20 gm. – Cholesterol: 70 mg. – Fiber: low

Olive Nut Spread

This flavorful low-fat spread can be used on crackers or pita bread squares for an appetizer or spread it on a bagel or bread for lunch. If regular mayonnaise and regular cream cheese were used in this recipe, each serving would have 200 calories and 20 grams of fat.

8 ounces fat-free cream cheese, room
    temperature
1/4 cup fat-free mayonnaise
1 tablespoon olive juice
1/4 teaspoon white pepper

1/2 cup green olives, chopped
1/2 cup black olives, chopped
1/2 cup pecans, chopped
dash Tabasco sauce
pecans for garnish

In a small bowl combine cream cheese, mayonnaise, and olive juice. Stir with a wooden spoon until smooth. Add extra olive juice if necessary to make a smooth, spreadable mixture. Stir in white pepper, olives, and pecans. Add Tabasco sauce to taste. Spoon into small serving bowl and garnish with pecans.

Makes 2 cups.

Note: Use all green or all black olives if you prefer.

Serves 8

Nutrition Information per serving:
Calories: 70 – Fat: 4 gm. – Protein: 5 gm.
Carbohydrate: 4 gm. – Cholesterol: 10 mg. – Fiber: low

Shrimp on Rye

 Shrimp seasoned with garlic and dill weed makes a special appetizer. The best part of this recipe is that you can make it ahead of time.

1 tablespoon butter or margarine

1/2 pound small shrimp, peeled and deveined

1 teaspoon lemon zest

1 tablespoon dill weed

1 clove garlic, minced

1 cup grated low-fat Swiss cheese

1/2 cup fat-free mayonnaise

1/8 teaspoon white pepper

12 slices cocktail rye bread

In a small skillet melt butter. Cook shrimp, lemon zest, dill weed, and garlic over medium-low heat about 5 minutes or until shrimp are pink and are cooked through. Let cool to room temperature. In a small bowl, combine cheese, mayonnaise, and white pepper. Add shrimp and stir gently. Cover and refrigerate until ready to use. Keeps up to 3 days.

When ready to serve, preheat oven broiler. Place cocktail rye bread on a baking sheet. Top each bread slice with a heaping teaspoon of shrimp mixture. Broil until puffed and golden, about 3 to 5 minutes. Watch carefully to prevent burning. Serve warm.

Serves 6 (2 slices per serving)

Nutrition Information per serving:
Calories: 185 – Fat: 5 gm. – Protein: 12 gm.
Carbohydrate: 37 gm. – Cholesterol: 70 mg. – Fiber: low

Spinach Bars

 Make these ahead and serve in small squares for an appetizer or serve in larger portions for a meatless meal.

1 tablespoon butter or margarine

1 medium onion, finely chopped

2 cloves garlic, minced

2 eggs

1/2 cup flour

1/2 teaspoon baking powder

1/3 cup milk

1/2 teaspoon salt

1/2 teaspoon oregano

1/8 teaspoon thyme

1/8 teaspoon marjoram

10 ounces frozen chopped spinach, thawed
    and squeezed dry

2 cups grated low-fat Monterey Jack or
    cheddar cheese, divided

Preheat oven to 325°. Grease an 8 x 8 inch baking pan. In a small skillet melt butter. Cook onions over medium heat until translucent. Add garlic; reduce heat and cook 1 minute. Set aside. In a large bowl beat eggs and add flour, baking powder, milk, salt, oregano, thyme, and marjoram. Stir in dry spinach and 1 1/2 cups of the cheese. Add onion and garlic. Stir to mix well. Pour mixture in pan. Top with remaining cheese. At this point it can be covered and stored in the refrigerator. Bake 30 to 40 minutes or until knife inserted near the middle comes out clean. (It will take longer to bake if it's been refrigerated.)

Cut into 16 small squares for an appetizer (2 squares per serving).

Serves 8

Nutrition Information per serving:
Calories: 145 – Fat: 7 gm. – Protein: 11 gm.
Carbohydrate: 9 gm. – Cholesterol: 50 mg. – Fiber: low

Superb Mushroom Spread

 When you serve this recipe for company, be ready to give out the recipe. Mushrooms blended with a hint of cayenne pepper and Worcestershire make a very special appetizer served on crackers. My husband liked it so well that he requested I serve it over noodles for a meal.

4 slices bacon

1 tablespoon bacon drippings

1 large onion, chopped

1 clove garlic, minced

1 1/2 pounds mushrooms, sliced

8 ounces low-fat cream cheese,
   room temperature

1 tablespoon Worcestershire sauce

1 tablespoon soy sauce

1/4 teaspoon cayenne pepper

1 cup fat-free sour cream

salt and freshly ground pepper to taste

In a large heavy frying pan, fry bacon until crisp. Remove from pan and crumble; set aside. Discard all but 1 tablespoon of the bacon drippings. Cook onions over medium heat in 1 tablespoon bacon drippings until onions are translucent. Add garlic and cook 1 minute. Add sliced mushrooms to the pan and cook until soft. Add cream cheese, stirring until melted and blended with mushrooms. Add Worcestershire sauce, soy sauce, and cayenne pepper. This can be place in a covered bowl and refrigerated until ready to serve.

When ready to serve, add sour cream and heat gently. Add salt and pepper to taste. Do not boil. If it is too thick, thin mixture with extra sour cream or a small amount of milk. Serve warm with crackers.

Serves 10

Nutrition Information per serving:
Calories: 125 — Fat: 7 gm. — Protein: 5 gm.
Carbohydrate: 10 gm. — Cholesterol: 20 mg. — Fiber: low

Toasted French Bread with Fresh Tomato Basil

 Also known as crostini. Refreshing, light appetizer or snack with zesty fresh flavor.

2 cups ripe tomatoes, seeded and chopped

2 cloves garlic, minced

1/4 cup fresh basil, minced, or 2 teaspoons dry basil

1/4 cup fresh parsley, minced

1 teaspoon sugar

1/2 teaspoon freshly ground pepper

1/2 teaspoon salt

2 tablespoons olive oil

1/2 loaf French bread, cut in 1-inch slices

butter-flavored cooking spray

1/4 teaspoon garlic powder

In a small bowl, combine tomatoes, garlic, basil, parsley, sugar, pepper, salt, and olive oil. Mix well. Spoon into serving bowl. Cover and refrigerate.

Preheat oven broiler. Place slices of French bread on baking pan. Spray bread with butter-flavored cooking spray and sprinkle with garlic powder. Turn and repeat on the other side. Broil until lightly browned on one side; turn and brown the other side. Watch carefully to prevent burning. Cool and set aside. When ready to serve, drain off excess liquid from tomato topping and discard. Place mixture in a bowl and serve toasted bread on a platter around the side. Spoon tomato mixture on top of bread and enjoy!

Serves 4

Nutrition Information per serving:
Calories: 100 – Fat: 7 gm. – Protein: 1 gm.
Carbohydrate: 8 – Cholesterol: 0 mg. – Fiber: low

White Bean Dip

 Add onions and garlic with a touch of wine vinegar to mild-flavored beans. Serve with fresh vegetables or tortilla chips.

1/2 cup green onions, chopped

3 cloves garlic, minced

2 tablespoons olive oil

30-ounce can white beans, drained

1 tablespoon lemon juice

2 tablespoons white wine vinegar

1/2 teaspoon freshly ground pepper

salt to taste

dash cayenne pepper, optional

1 tablespoon minced fresh cilantro

In a medium skillet over low heat, cook onions and garlic in oil until onions are translucent. Add beans, lemon juice, white wine vinegar, and pepper. Place mixture in food processor and process until smooth. Add salt to taste. Add cayenne pepper if desired. Stir in cilantro. Serve warm or at room temperature with fresh vegetables, crackers, or tortilla chips.

12 servings

Nutrition Information per serving:
Calories: 100 – Fat: 2 gm. – Protein: 5 gm.
Carbohydrate: 16 – Cholesterol: 0 mg. – Fiber: high

Salads

Apple & Grape Salad with Peach Yogurt Dressing

Fruit with touches of honey, allspice, and nutmeg. It is so good!

1 teaspoon honey

1 tablespoon lemon juice

2 large apples, cored and diced

6 ounces fat-free peach yogurt

1/4 cup fat-free mayonnaise

1/4 teaspoon allspice

1/8 teaspoon nutmeg

1 stalk celery, diced

2 cups (1 pound) fresh seedless purple
   grapes

In a large bowl, combine honey and lemon juice. Add apples and mix well.

In a small bowl mix yogurt, mayonnaise, allspice, and nutmeg. Add dressing to apples. Stir in celery and grapes. Cover and chill.

Serves 8

Nutrition Information per serving:
Calories: 75 — Fat: 0 gm. — Protein: 1 gm.
Carbohydrate: 18 — Cholesterol: 0 mg. — Fiber: medium

Apple Walnut Salad with Cranberry Vinaigrette

 A very special tangy dressing with the bite of mustard powder and the sweetness of honey and allspice.

1 teaspoon dry mustard	**Dressing:**
1/4 cup water	1/4 cup fresh cranberries
3 large red apples, cored and diced	1/4 cup balsamic vinegar
1 tablespoon lemon juice	1/4 cup finely chopped red onion
2 teaspoons honey	2 tablespoons sugar
6 cups leaf lettuce, torn	1/4 cup extra virgin olive oil
	1/8 teaspoon allspice
	1/2 cup toasted walnuts

In a small custard cup, combine mustard and water. Stir until smooth. Set aside. In a large salad bowl, combine apples with lemon juice and honey. Add lettuce. Set aside. In a blender combine cranberries, vinegar, onion, sugar, olive oil, allspice, and reserved mustard mixture. Mix dressing with lettuce and apples. Sprinkle with walnuts.

Serves 8

Nutrition Information per serving:
Calories: 150 – Fat: 8 gm. – Protein: 2 gm.
Carbohydrate: 17 – Cholesterol: 0 mg. – Fiber: high

Belgian Tomatoes

 A flavorful way to serve fresh tomatoes and onions with basil and dill weed.

1/3 cup fat-free French dressing

1/4 teaspoon white pepper

1/4 teaspoon dill weed

1/4 teaspoon basil

1/4 teaspoon salt

1/2 teaspoon sugar

2 large fresh tomatoes, sliced

1/2 large sweet onion, thinly sliced

1/3 cup grated Romano or Parmesan cheese

In a small bowl, combine French dressing, white pepper, dill weed, basil, salt, and sugar. Set aside. Arrange one layer of tomato slices in a 9-inch round serving bowl. Place half of the onion slices on top. Drizzle with half of the dressing mixture. Repeat with another layer of tomatoes and onion slices. Drizzle with remaining dressing. Sprinkle grated cheese on top. Cover and refrigerate several hours.

Serves 4

Nutrition Information per serving:
Calories: 80 – Fat: 2 gm. – Protein: 4 gm.
Carbohydrate: 11 – Cholesterol: 0 mg. – Fiber: medium

Carrot Raisin Salad with Cinnamon Honey Dressing

What an enjoyable way to eat your carrots!

5 large carrots

3/4 cup fat-free mayonnaise

2 tablespoons honey

2 teaspoons cider vinegar

1/2 teaspoon cinnamon

dash salt

1/2 cup golden raisins

1/4 cup dry-roasted peanuts (optional)

Peel carrots. Grate carrots or process in a food processor until coarsely grated. (You should have about 4 cups grated carrots.) In a small bowl, combine mayonnaise, honey, vinegar, cinnamon, and salt. In a large bowl, combine grated carrots, dressing, and raisins. Refrigerate until ready to serve. Top with dry-roasted peanuts, if desired, just before serving.

Serves 6

Nutrition Information per serving:
Calories: 140 – Fat: 2 gm. – Protein: 3 gm.
Carbohydrate: 27 – Cholesterol: 0 mg. – Fiber: high

Chicken Caesar Salad

 Caesar salads can be loaded with calories and fat but this slimmed down version has a wonderful, full flavor.

1/2 cup fat-free sour cream

1/2 cup fat-free mayonnaise

1 teaspoon Dijon mustard

1 clove garlic, finely minced

2 teaspoons red wine vinegar

1/2 teaspoon anchovy paste

1/4 teaspoon white pepper

2 tablespoons grated Parmesan cheese

1/4 cup fat-free milk

6 boneless chicken breast halves without skin

1/2 teaspoon salt

1/4 teaspoon pepper

1/4 teaspoon paprika

1 tablespoon cooking oil

1 bunch romaine lettuce

1/2 cup freshly grated Parmesan cheese

freshly ground pepper to taste

Prepare dressing: In a medium bowl, combine sour cream, mayonnaise, mustard, garlic, vinegar, anchovy paste, white pepper, and 2 tablespoons grated Parmesan cheese. Add skim milk to thin. Cover and refrigerate. Sprinkle chicken breasts with salt, pepper, and paprika. Heat oil in large skillet. Fry chicken breasts over medium heat until brown on both sides and completely done in the middle. Remove from pan and cut into thin slices. In a large salad bowl, tear lettuce into bite-sized pieces. Add dressing and toss until lettuce is well coated. Divide lettuce onto 6 individual serving plates. Arrange chicken breast pieces on top of lettuce. Top salad with Parmesan cheese and pepper.

Serves 6

Nutrition Information per serving:
Calories: 200 – Fat: 6 gm. – Protein: 31 gm.
Carbohydrate: 6 gm. – Cholesterol: 70 mg. – Fiber: medium

Couscous and Vegetable Salad

 This salad is beautiful, colorful, and light.
It's best with fresh basil.

3/4 cup uncooked couscous

2 tablespoons extra virgin olive oil

2 tablespoons white wine vinegar

1/4 cup minced fresh basil or 1 teaspoon
    dry basil

1/4 cup fresh parsley, minced

1 clove garlic, minced

1/2 teaspoon salt

1/2 teaspoon freshly ground pepper

1 large tomato, seeded and chopped

1 small zucchini, cut in thin strips

1 small red pepper, cut in thin strips

4 green onions, sliced

1/4 cup pitted black olives, sliced

Prepare couscous according to package directions. In a large bowl, combine olive oil, vinegar, basil, parsley, garlic, salt, and pepper. Mix well. Add tomato, zucchini, pepper, onions, and olives. Stir gently. Add couscous and stir until well blended. Serve at room temperature or cover and refrigerate until ready to serve.

Note: This salad is especially attractive served in a shiny, dark colored pottery bowl.

Serves 6

Nutrition Information per serving:
Calories: 175 – Fat: 5 gm. – Protein: 5 gm.
Carbohydrate: 28 – Cholesterol: 0 mg. – Fiber: high

Cranberry Waldorf Salad

 The cranberries add the unusual zest.

1 cup fresh cranberries, chopped

3 large apples, cored and diced

2 stalks celery, diced

2/3 cup fat-free mayonnaise

1/3 cup fat-free sour cream

3 tablespoons lemon juice

3 tablespoons sugar

1/4 teaspoon cinnamon

1/4 teaspoon nutmeg

3/4 cup walnuts, chopped

Combine cranberries, apples, and celery. In a small bowl combine mayonnaise, sour cream, lemon juice, sugar, cinnamon, and nutmeg. Spoon dressing into fruit and mix well. Refrigerate. When ready to serve add nuts.

Serves 6

Nutrition Information per serving:
Calories: 105 – Fat: 2 gm. – Protein: 1 gm.
Carbohydrate: 21 gm. – Cholesterol: 2 mg. – Fiber: high

Danish Mushroom Salad

 If you are a mushroom lover, you will love this recipe.
It makes mushrooms so special.

1 1/2 pounds fresh mushrooms, sliced

2 cups water

2 tablespoons lemon juice

1/2 teaspoon salt

1/2 cup fat-free sour cream

4 small green onions, minced

1 teaspoon lemon juice

1/2 teaspoon sugar

1/8 teaspoon nutmeg

1/4 teaspoon salt

freshly ground pepper to taste

4 lettuce leaves

Place mushrooms in a medium skillet. Add water, lemon juice, and salt. Bring to a boil and cook for 1 minute or just until mushrooms are beginning to be tender. Drain well and pat dry. In a medium bowl combine sour cream, onions, lemon juice, sugar, nutmeg, salt, and pepper. Add mushrooms and stir gently. Refrigerate until ready to serve. Serve on lettuce leaves.

Serves 4

Nutrition Information per serving:
Calories: 100 – Fat: 0 gm. – Protein: 6 gm.
Carbohydrate: 19 – Cholesterol: 0 mg. – Fiber: high

Guiltless Potato Salad

 This recipe is a real surprise— it's well worth a try! It's low in fat and calories but tastes just like the regular high-calorie potato salad. The blend of seasonings makes the difference.

3 pounds small red potatoes

1 medium red onion, diced

1/2 cup diced celery

3 tablespoons fat-free French dressing

1/2 cup fat-free mayonnaise

1/2 tablespoon Durkees Famous Sauce

1 tablespoon Dijon mustard

dash Tabasco sauce

1/4 teaspoon white pepper

salt to taste

In a saucepan, boil red potatoes just until fork tender. (Do not overcook.) Quarter the potatoes. In a large bowl, combine warm potatoes with diced onions and celery. Gently stir 2 to 3 tablespoons of French dressing into potatoes and marinate for an hour at room temperature. Set aside. In a small bowl, combine mayonnaise, Durkees sauce, mustard, Tabasco, white pepper, and salt. Taste the dressing and add more mustard or seasonings to suit your taste. Combine dressing with potatoes. Refrigerate until ready to serve.

Serves 4

Nutrition Information per serving:
Calories: 250 – Fat: 0.5 gm. – Protein: 6 gm.
Carbohydrate: 55 – Cholesterol: 0 mg. – Fiber: high

Ham and Apple Salad

 Nutmeg and cloves are a winning combination with apples and ham.

1/2 cup fat-free mayonnaise

1 teaspoon Dijon mustard

2 teaspoons honey

2 teaspoons lemon juice

1/4 teaspoon nutmeg

1/8 teaspoon cloves

2 cups diced cooked ham

2 apples, cored and diced

2 stalks celery, diced

1 1/2 cups canned pineapple chunks, drained

1 teaspoon toasted sesame seeds

Combine mayonnaise, mustard, honey, lemon juice, nutmeg, and cloves. Stir in ham, apples, celery, and pineapple. Sprinkle with toasted sesame seeds right before serving.

Serves 4

Nutrition Information per serving:
Calories: 200 – Fat: 4 gm. – Protein: 14 gm.
Carbohydrate: 28 gm. – Cholesterol: 30 mg. – Fiber: medium

Marinated Tomatoes and Cucumbers

 Tomatoes are special—full of the phytochemical lycopene. Make it easy to serve them often by preparing ahead with basil and garlic.

4 large ripe tomatoes, sliced

2 large cucumbers, peeled and sliced

1 large sweet onion, sliced

1/4 cup extra virgin olive oil

1/4 cup red wine vinegar

2 tablespoons minced fresh parsley

1 clove garlic, minced

2 tablespoons minced fresh basil
    or 2 teaspoons dry basil

1/4 teaspoon salt

1/4 teaspoon freshly ground black pepper

2 tablespoons capers, optional

Arrange tomato slices, cucumber slices, and onion slices in a zipping plastic bag. In a small bowl, combine olive oil, vinegar, parsley, garlic, basil, salt, pepper, and capers. Pour over vegetables. Mix gently. Refrigerate several hours or overnight. Discard extra dressing before serving.

Serves 6

Nutrition Information per serving:
Calories: 80 – Fat: 4 gm. – Protein: 2 gm.
Carbohydrate: 9 – Cholesterol: 0 mg. – Fiber: low

Mediterranean Tuna Salad

 This is an adaptation of the traditional Niçoise salad. The rosemary and dill weed are essential seasonings in the dressing.

4 new red potatoes

4 cups leaf lettuce

4 cups fresh spinach leaves

1 medium red onion, thinly sliced

6-ounce can white tuna, drained,
    or fresh grilled tuna

1 cup canned or cooked fresh green beans

4 Roma tomatoes, quartered

12 pitted black olives

freshly ground pepper to taste

Dressing:

1/4 cup white wine vinegar

3 tablespoons extra virgin olive oil

2 teaspoons Dijon mustard

1/8 teaspoon dill weed

1/4 teaspoon rosemary, crushed

1/4 teaspoon freshly ground pepper

2 tablespoons minced fresh parsley

Boil potatoes just until fork tender. Cool and cut into 1/2-inch slices. Line 4 plates with lettuce and spinach leaves. Arrange potatoes, onions, tuna, beans, tomatoes, and olives attractively on lettuce. In a small jar, mix together dressing ingredients. Shake until well mixed. Pour dressing over salad. Serve with freshly ground pepper to taste.

Note: It is important to crush the rosemary. A mortar and pestle work well to crush spices and herbs.

Serves 4

Nutrition Information per serving:
Calories: 290 – Fat: 13 gm. – Protein: 16 gm.
Carbohydrate: 28 gm. – Cholesterol: 20 mg. – Fiber: high

Orange, Strawberry, Spinach Salad with Cinnamon Honey Dressing

This colorful salad has just the right mix of sweet and sour taste.

2 medium oranges	2 tablespoons honey
1 cup fresh strawberries	2 tablespoons raspberry vinegar
5 ounces fresh spinach	1/2 teaspoon cinnamon
2 tablespoons corn or canola oil	1 tablespoon pine nuts, toasted (optional)

Peel oranges and remove membrane from sections. Cut sections in half. Wash strawberries, remove hulls, and cut in half. Wash spinach, dry thoroughly, and tear into pieces. Discard tough stem parts. In a large salad bowl, combine oranges, strawberries, and spinach. In a small bowl, mix together oil, honey, raspberry vinegar, and cinnamon. Add to fruit and spinach and toss. Top with pine nuts if desired.

Serves 4

Nutrition Information per serving:
Calories: 160 – Fat: 7 gm. – Protein: 2 gm.
Carbohydrate: 23 – Cholesterol: 0 mg. – Fiber: high

Prairie Country Salad

 This salad is fresh and crunchy.

3 cups broccoli florets

3 cups cauliflower florets

1/2 cup golden raisins

1/2 small red onion, sliced

6 strips bacon, fried and crumbled

1/2 cup sunflower seeds, toasted

Dressing:

1 cup fat-free mayonnaise

1/3 cup sugar

1/4 cup apple cider vinegar

1/4 teaspoon allspice

Blanch broccoli florets in a pan of boiling water for 1 minute. Chill quickly under cold running water. Drain and pat dry. In a large bowl, combine broccoli, cauliflower, raisins, onions, and fried bacon. In a small jar, mix together mayonnaise, sugar, vinegar, and allspice. Pour dressing over salad and toss. Refrigerate for several hours before serving. Add sunflower seeds right before serving.

Serves 6

Nutrition Information per serving:
Calories: 190 – Fat: 5 gm. – Protein: 5 gm.
Carbohydrate: 32 gm. – Cholesterol: 5 mg. – Fiber: high

Raspberry Vinaigrette Green Salad with Macadamia Nuts

 Tasty and elegant. The raspberry vinegar with honey and allspice is absolutely wonderful served with leaf lettuce, raspberries, and nuts.

1/2 cup raspberry vinegar

1 tablespoon Dijon mustard

1/4 cup sugar

2 tablespoons honey

1/4 teaspoon allspice

3 tablespoons olive oil

1/4 teaspoon freshly ground pepper

12 cups torn lettuce leaves

2 cups fresh raspberries or loose pack frozen raspberries

1/3 cup macadamia nuts

Combine vinegar, mustard, sugar, honey, allspice, oil, and pepper in a small jar. Shake to mix well. In a large salad bowl combine lettuce, raspberries, nuts, and dressing. Toss.

Note: Substitute nuts of your choice for the macadamia nuts.

Serves 6

Nutrition Information per serving:
Calories: 175 – Fat: 9 gm. – Protein: 2 gm.
Carbohydrate: 22 – Cholesterol: 0 mg. – Fiber: high

Spinach Salad with Honey Orange Dressing

 Coriander and cilantro are combined in this light, refreshing orange-lime dressing.

8 cups fresh spinach

1 medium orange, peeled, sectioned, and diced

1 medium red onion, thinly sliced

Dressing:

1/2 cup orange juice

2 tablespoons lime juice

2 tablespoons extra virgin olive oil

2 tablespoons honey

1/4 teaspoon ground coriander

1/4 cup fresh cilantro, chopped

salt to taste

Wash spinach and dry thoroughly. Tear into bite-size pieces. In a large salad bowl, combine spinach with oranges and onions. Cover and refrigerate. In a small bowl, combine all dressing ingredients. Refrigerate until ready to serve. Toss dressing with spinach.

Serves 6

Nutrition Information per serving:
Calories: 110 – Fat: 5 gm. – Protein: 2 gm.
Carbohydrate: 14 – Cholesterol: 0 mg. – Fiber: medium

Spinach with Apples and Feta Cheese

 A healthy spinach salad. The dry mustard
in the dressing adds extra zip.

8 cups torn spinach

4 green onions, chopped

3 slices bacon

3 tablespoons bacon fat

3 tablespoons vinegar

3 tablespoons sugar

1/2 teaspoon dry mustard

2 red apples, sliced or chopped

2 ounces low-fat feta cheese, crumbled

1 hard-cooked egg, peeled and crumbled

freshly ground pepper

Wash spinach; drain well and combine with onions in large salad bowl. Set aside. In a medium skillet fry bacon until crisp. Remove bacon, reserving 3 tablespoons bacon drippings in skillet. Drain bacon on paper towels. Crumble bacon and set aside. Add vinegar, sugar, and dry mustard to the reserved drippings. Bring to a boil. Remove from heat and toss with spinach. Add apple slices and feta cheese. Toss lightly to mix. Top with egg and crumbled bacon. Serve immediately. Add freshly ground pepper to each serving.

Serves 6

Nutrition Information per serving:
Calories: 195 – Fat: 9 gm. – Protein: 6 gm.
Carbohydrate: 22 gm. – Cholesterol: 45 mg. – Fiber: high

Strawberry Kiwi Salad

 So attractive! Try to use fresh tarragon for the dressing.

6 cups torn tender leaf lettuce

1 pint fresh strawberries, hulled and sliced

5 medium kiwi fruit, peeled and sliced

Dressing:

1/4 cup honey

1/4 cup cider vinegar

2 tablespoons fresh tarragon

    or 2 teaspoons dried tarragon

2 tablespoons salad oil

In a large salad bowl combine lettuce, strawberries, and kiwi. Set aside.

In a small jar combine honey, vinegar, tarragon, and salad oil. Mix well. When ready to serve, drizzle dressing over salad ingredients.

Note: Other fruits such as bananas, grapes, and apples are also good with this dressing.

Serves 6

Nutrition Information per serving:
Calories: 185 – Fat: 7 gm. – Protein: 3 gm.
Carbohydrate: 29 – Cholesterol: 0 mg. – Fiber: high

Turkey and Wild Rice with Orange Marmalade Dressing

 An elegant luncheon dish. The orange-flavored dressing with a hint of nutmeg is perfect with wild rice and leftover turkey.

1 cup raw wild rice

3 cups salted water

2 pounds cooked turkey breast, cut in
    bite-sized pieces

3 medium apples, cored and diced

1 cup canned or fresh pineapple chunks

1/2 cup slivered almonds, toasted

Dressing:

1/2 cup orange marmalade

3/4 cup fat-free mayonnaise

1/4 cup fat-free sour cream

2 tablespoons lemon juice

1/4 teaspoon nutmeg

In a heavy saucepan, combine wild rice and salted water. Bring to a boil, cover, and simmer for about 45 minutes or until rice is tender. Drain and chill rice. In a large bowl, combine chilled rice with cooked turkey, diced apples, and pineapple. Cover and store in refrigerator. Prepare dressing by combining orange marmalade, mayonnaise, sour cream, lemon juice, and nutmeg in a small bowl. Cover and refrigerate until ready to use. When ready to serve, combine salad with dressing. Garnish with toasted almonds.

Note: Fresh grapes can be substituted for the pineapple.

Serves 8

Nutrition Information per serving:
Calories: 335 – Fat: 7 gm. – Protein: 29 gm.
Carbohydrate: 39 gm. – Cholesterol: 50 mg. – Fiber: medium

Wild Rice Salad

 This salad is colorful and has a subtle taste with the lemon juice, dill weed, and dry mustard in the dressing. It goes very well with a sandwich meal or a picnic.

1 cup long-grain wild rice mix

11-ounce can corn, drained

1/4 cup parsley, chopped

3 green onions, chopped

1 medium cucumber, peeled, seeded, and diced

2 medium carrots, peeled and finely chopped

1/4 cup lemon juice

1 tablespoon extra virgin olive oil

2 cloves garlic, minced

1 teaspoon dill weed

1/4 teaspoon freshly ground black pepper

1/2 teaspoon dry mustard

1/2 teaspoon salt

Prepare rice according to package directions, omitting fat. Cool rice.

In a large bowl, combine rice, corn, parsley, onions, cucumber, and carrots. In a small bowl, combine lemon juice, olive oil, garlic, dill weed, pepper, dry mustard, pepper, and salt. Pour over rice mixture, tossing gently. Adjust seasoning with extra salt and extra pepper to taste. Cover and refrigerate several hours.

Serves 6

Nutrition Information per serving:
Calories: 240 – Fat: 4 gm. – Protein: 6 gm.
Carbohydrate: 46 – Cholesterol: 0 mg. – Fiber: high

Breads

Cranberry Orange Nut Bread

 A beautiful quick bread made special with the flavor of cardamom and orange zest.

2 cups flour	2 tablespoons butter, melted
1/2 teaspoon salt	2 tablespoons hot water
1 1/2 teaspoons baking powder	1/3 cup orange juice
1/2 teaspoon baking soda	3 tablespoons lemon juice
1 cup sugar	1 tablespoon orange zest
1/2 teaspoon cardamom	1 cup cranberries
2 eggs, lightly beaten	1/2 cup walnuts, toasted

Preheat oven to 325°. Grease 9 x 15 inch loaf pan. In a large bowl, combine flour, salt, baking powder, baking soda, sugar, and cardamom. In another bowl beat eggs and add butter, water, orange juice, lemon juice, and orange zest. Combine dry ingredients and egg mixture. Stir until just mixed. Fold in cranberries and nuts. Pour batter into greased loaf pan. Bake for 1 hour or until light brown and a wooden pick inserted in the middle comes out clean. Remove from pan and cool on a rack.

Serve with Cinnamon-Sugar Butter (see page 212).

Serves 12

Nutrition Information per serving:
Calories: 180 – Fat: 3 gm. – Protein: 4 gm.
Carbohydrate: 35 gm. – Cholesterol: 35 mg. – Fiber: low

Fat-Free Bran Muffins

 Keep the batter in the refrigerator for weeks and have fresh, moist, tasty muffins ready in minutes.

2 1/2 cups All Bran cereal

3/4 cup boiling water

1/2 cup fruit puree (one brand is
    Just Like Shortenin')*

1/4 cup molasses

2 cups buttermilk

1 cup sugar

2 eggs

2 1/2 teaspoons baking soda

1 teaspoon salt

1/2 teaspoon cinnamon

1/2 teaspoon allspice

2 1/2 cups flour

Preheat oven to 375°. Grease 24 muffin tins. In a small bowl, mix cereal with the boiling water. Set aside. In a large bowl, combine fruit puree, molasses, buttermilk, sugar, and eggs. Beat together. Add baking soda, salt, cinnamon, allspice, and flour. Stir just until blended. Stir in the moistened cereal. Fill greased muffin tins 3/4 full. Bake for 15 to 20 minutes or until lightly browned. Do not overbake.

Note: Add nuts or raisins to the batter before baking if desired. The dough can be stored in a covered bowl in the refrigerator for up to 6 weeks.

*Distributed by the Plum Life Company, Madison, CT

Serves 24

Nutrition Information per serving:
Calories: 130 – Fat: <1 gm. – Protein: 4 gm.
Carbohydrate: 30 gm. – Cholesterol: 15 mg. – Fiber: medium

Herb Garlic Bread

 Enjoy the fragrance of garlic and thyme.

3 cloves garlic, finely minced

1/4 cup olive oil

1/4 cup fresh parsley, finely chopped

1/2 teaspoon thyme

1 teaspoon marjoram

1 teaspoon paprika

1 loaf French bread

1/2 cup grated Parmesan cheese

Preheat oven broiler. Combine garlic, olive oil, parsley, thyme, marjoram, and paprika in a custard cup. Cut French bread in half lengthwise. Brush each half with garlic-oil mixture. Sprinkle grated cheese on top. Place under broiler until brown. Watch carefully to prevent burning.

Serves 10

Nutrition Information per serving:
Calories: 190 – Fat: 8 gm. – Protein: 6 gm.
Carbohydrate: 24 gm. – Cholesterol: 5 mg. – Fiber: low

Oatmeal Muffins

 The cinnamon and sugar top off a muffin with a homemade aroma and taste. What a great way to enjoy oatmeal!

1 cup oatmeal	1 teaspoon baking powder
1 cup buttermilk	1 teaspoon baking soda
1/3 cup butter or margarine	1/2 teaspoon salt
1/2 cup brown sugar	1/2 teaspoon cardamom
1 egg	1 teaspoon cinnamon
2 cups flour	1/4 teaspoon sugar

Preheat oven to 400°. Grease 14 muffin tins. In a small bowl combine oatmeal and buttermilk. Set aside. In a medium bowl beat butter and brown sugar together. Add egg and beat well. Stir in the oatmeal and milk. Combine flour, baking powder, baking soda, salt, and cardamom. Stir dry ingredients into oatmeal mixture. Stir gently and as little as possible. (Vigorous stirring makes tough muffins.) Spoon into muffin pan, filling 2/3 full. Bake for 15 to 20 minutes until lightly browned. While baking, combine cinnamon and sugar in a custard cup or a shaker. Remove muffins from the tin. Cool on a rack. Sprinkle with cinnamon and sugar mixture.

Note: This mixture can be stored in the refrigerator until ready to bake.

Serve with Cinnamon-Sugar Butter (see page 212).

Serves 14

Nutrition Information per serving:
Calories: 150 – Fat: 5 gm. – Protein: 4 gm.
Carbohydrate: 23 gm. – Cholesterol: 25 mg. – Fiber: low

Rhubarb Muffins

 A muffin so moist with the warm taste of allspice.

1 1/2 cups brown sugar

1 1/4 cups buttermilk

1/2 cup vegetable oil

1 egg

2 teaspoons vanilla

2 cups rhubarb, diced in small pieces

2 1/2 cups flour

1 teaspoon baking powder

1 teaspoon baking soda

1/2 teaspoon salt

1/4 teaspoon nutmeg

1/2 teaspoon allspice

Preheat oven to 375°. Grease 18 muffin tins. In a large bowl, combine brown sugar, buttermilk, vegetable oil, egg, and vanilla. Beat well. Stir in the rhubarb. Sift together flour, baking powder, baking soda, salt, nutmeg, and allspice. Add to egg mixture and stir gently just until blended. Do not overmix. Spoon batter into muffin tins, filling 3/4 full. Bake for 20 to 25 minutes or until lightly browned. Remove muffins from pan and cool on a rack.

Serve with Cinnamon-Sugar Butter (see page 212).

Serves 18

Nutrition Information per muffin:
Calories: 170 – Fat: 6 gm. – Protein: 3 gm.
Carbohydrate: 26 gm. – Cholesterol: 10 mg. – Fiber: very low

Saffron Bread with Cardamom Honey

 A basic bread machine recipe. If you have a bread machine, you have your favorite standard recipes. But try this one that is so unusual. It is slightly yellow and has that subtle special saffron taste.

3 1/3 cups bread flour

2 tablespoons sugar

1 1/2 tablespoons dry fat-free milk

1 1/2 teaspoons salt

small pinch saffron, about 20 threads

small pinch cardamom

1 1/2 tablespoons butter or margarine

1 3/8 cups water

1 1/2 teaspoons dry yeast

Combine first six dry ingredients in bread machine pan. Add butter and water. Add yeast according to machine directions. Bake according to machine directions.

Serve with cardamom honey (recipe follows).

Serves 12

Nutrition Information per serving:
Calories: 160 – Fat: 2 gm. – Protein: 5 gm.
Carbohydrate: 31 gm. – Cholesterol: 5 mg. – Fiber: low

Cardamom Honey

 So good on fresh bread, biscuits, toast, or waffles.

1/2 cup honey

dash of cardamom

Mix honey and add cardamom to taste.

Vegetables

Acorn Squash Stuffed with Apples and Dried Cranberries

 The blend of red cranberries and apples combined with cinnamon and brown sugar is colorful and delicious. Serve it for family or company meals.

2 small acorn squash, cut in half	1/2 teaspoon salt
1 tablespoon butter or margarine, melted	1/3 cup dried cranberries
1/2 teaspoon cinnamon	2 medium apples, cored and diced
1/2 teaspoon allspice	1/3 cup brown sugar

Preheat oven to 375°. Clean seeds from squash and discard seeds. Arrange squash halves cut-side up in a 9 x 9 inch baking pan. Pour water in the pan about an inch deep. Set aside. In a medium bowl combine melted butter, cinnamon, allspice, salt, cranberries, apples, and brown sugar. Spoon apple mixture into squash halves. Cover pan with aluminum foil. Bake for 45 to 60 minutes or until squash is tender. Serve in small individual bowls.

Serves 4

Nutrition Information per serving:
Calories: 180 – Fat: 3 gm. – Protein: 1 gm.
Carbohydrate: 38 gm. – Cholesterol: 10 mg. – Fiber: high

Asparagus with Orange Ginger Sauce

 Ginger and orange make asparagus even more special.

1 tablespoon butter or margarine	1/2 teaspoon cornstarch
1/8 teaspoon ground ginger	1 teaspoon brown sugar
1/4 teaspoon allspice	1 pound fresh or frozen asparagus
1/4 teaspoon salt	1 teaspoon orange zest
1/4 cup orange juice	4 thin orange slices

In a small saucepan melt butter. Add ginger, allspice, and salt. Stir to mix. In a small custard cup combine orange juice, cornstarch, and brown sugar. Add to saucepan. Bring to a boil, stirring constantly until mixture thickens. Remove from heat and set aside. In a large saucepan cook asparagus in salted boiling water until tender-crisp. Drain well. Arrange on serving plates. Drizzle with warm sauce. Top with orange zest and orange slices.

Note: If asparagus is not available, try this sauce on a mixture of green beans, yellow beans, and carrots.

Serves 4

Nutrition Information per serving:
Calories: 55 – Fat: 3 gm. – Protein: 1 gm.
Carbohydrate: 6 gm. – Cholesterol: 10 mg. – Fiber: low

Baby Carrots and Brussels Sprouts with Zesty Lemon Sauce

 This lemon sauce seasoned with dill weed can be prepared ahead of time and refrigerated. When ready to serve, warm the sauce and combine with cooked vegetables.

1 pound Brussels sprouts

1/2 pound baby carrots

Sauce:

1 tablespoon extra virgin olive oil

1/8 teaspoon salt

1/4 cup fresh lemon juice

1/4 teaspoon freshly ground black pepper

1 teaspoon lemon zest

1/2 teaspoon dill weed

2 tablespoons honey

2 tablespoons fresh parsley, minced

1 tablespoon fat-free mayonnaise

Cook Brussels sprouts in a small saucepan about 6 to 8 minutes or until bright green and crisp-tender. Cook carrots in another small saucepan about 8 to 10 minutes or until crisp-tender. Drain vegetables and place in a warm serving dish. While vegetables are cooking, combine all sauce ingredients in a small jar; shake well. Heat sauce in a small saucepan or in the microwave. Toss hot vegetables together with warm sauce.

Serves 4

Nutrition Information per serving:
Calories: 150 – Fat: 4 gm. – Protein: 4 gm.
Carbohydrate: 24 – Cholesterol: 0 mg. – Fiber: high

Baked Onions and Potatoes Parmesan

 If you like potatoes you will love these potatoes seasoned with freshly ground pepper and Parmesan cheese. It is also wonderful prepared with other cheeses such as cheddar, Monterey Jack, or Swiss.

3 tablespoons butter or margarine

2 jumbo onions, thinly sliced

1/2 teaspoon salt

1/2 teaspoon freshly ground pepper

4 large potatoes, peeled and thinly sliced

1 cup fresh grated Parmesan cheese

1/4 teaspoon paprika

Preheat oven to 350°. Butter a 2-quart casserole dish. In a medium heavy skillet melt butter. Add onions and cook over medium heat for 10 to 15 minutes until onions become caramelized or light brown. Stir in salt and pepper. Arrange a third of the potato slices in the casserole dish. Top with a third of the onions and a third of the Parmesan cheese. Repeat layers two more times. Sprinkle paprika on top. Bake for 60 to 70 minutes or until potatoes are tender and crusty brown on top.

Note: This recipe will not work well with the dried grated Parmesan cheese. Other fresh cheese may be substituted for the Parmesan cheese if desired.

Serves 6

Nutrition Information per serving:
Calories: 165 – Fat: 10 gm. – Protein: 7 gm.
Carbohydrate: 12 gm. – Cholesterol: 25 mg. – Fiber: medium

Basil Roasted Potatoes

 Add spice to the life of ordinary baked potatoes.

vegetable oil cooking spray

4 large unpeeled potatoes, sliced lengthwise
    into 8 pieces

2 tablespoons olive oil

1 teaspoon sugar

1/4 teaspoon garlic powder

1/4 teaspoon paprika

1/2 teaspoon basil

1/2 teaspoon freshly ground pepper

dash cayenne pepper

1/2 teaspoon salt

Preheat oven to 375°. Spray a heavy baking pan with cooking spray. Place potato slices in large resealable plastic bag. Add olive oil, sugar, garlic powder, paprika, basil, pepper, cayenne pepper, and salt. Reseal bag and mix well. Remove potatoes from bag and arrange potatoes one layer thick on the baking pan. Bake for 20 minutes; turn potatoes. Bake an additional 15 to 20 minutes or until lightly browned and very tender.

Serves 4

Nutrition Information per serving:
Calories: 160 – Fat: 7 gm. – Protein: 3 gm.
Carbohydrate: 23 – Cholesterol: 0 mg. – Fiber: low

Brussels Sprouts with Water Chestnuts and Bacon

 Bacon has a bad reputation but it has only 60 calories and 5 grams of fat in a 2-slice serving. It can add great flavor even in small amounts.

4 slices bacon, diced	1/4 teaspoon nutmeg
4-ounce can water chestnuts	1/4 teaspoon white pepper
1 pound Brussels sprouts	1/4 cup seasoned dry bread crumbs
1/2 cup chicken broth	2 tablespoons freshly grated Parmesan cheese

Preheat oven to 325°. Butter a 1-quart casserole dish. In a small skillet fry bacon until crisp. Remove bacon from pan and set aside. Add water chestnuts to skillet and cook over low heat for 2 minutes. Remove from pan and drain on a paper towel. Discard bacon grease. Cook Brussels sprouts in salted water just until crisp-tender. Drain. Combine Brussels sprouts with water chestnuts and bacon and spoon into casserole dish. Mix chicken broth, nutmeg, and white pepper. Pour over vegetables. Sprinkle with bread crumbs and Parmesan cheese. Bake 10 to 15 minutes or until vegetables are hot and top is light brown.

Serves 4

Nutrition Information per serving:
Calories: 120 – Fat: 4 gm. – Protein: 7 gm.
Carbohydrate: 14 gm. – Cholesterol: 10 mg. – Fiber: high

Cauliflower with Parmesan

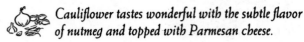 *Cauliflower tastes wonderful with the subtle flavor of nutmeg and topped with Parmesan cheese.*

2 cloves garlic, minced

1 tablespoon butter or margarine

1/3 cup low-fat chicken broth

1/2 teaspoon nutmeg

1/8 teaspoon freshly ground pepper

1/2 teaspoon salt

1/4 cup bread crumbs

4 cups cauliflower florets

1/3 cup freshly grated Parmesan cheese

1/4 teaspoon paprika

In a small saucepan, cook garlic in butter over low heat for about 1 minute or until garlic is soft. Add chicken broth, nutmeg, pepper, and salt. Bring to a boil; reduce heat and simmer for 3 minutes. Set aside. Place bread crumbs in a small nonstick skillet and stir over medium heat until toasted. Set aside. Cook cauliflower in a large pot of boiling salted water about 5 to 7 minutes or until crisp-tender. Do not overcook. Drain well. Pour chicken broth mixture over cauliflower and mix gently. Place in serving bowl and top with bread crumbs and Parmesan cheese. Sprinkle with paprika.

Serves 4

Nutrition Information per serving:
Calories: 100 – Fat: 6 gm. – Protein: 4 gm.
Carbohydrate: 7 gm. – Cholesterol: 10 mg. – Fiber: very low

Creamed Cabbage

 This is one vegetable you won't often find on a restaurant menu but it is so good. The dry mustard, white pepper, and thyme in a white sauce give it the appealing country taste.

2 pounds cabbage (1 small head), chopped	1/2 teaspoon dry mustard
1 tablespoon butter or margarine	1/8 teaspoon white pepper
1 tablespoon flour	1/4 teaspoon thyme
1/2 cup fat-free milk	salt to taste
1/2 cup chicken broth	freshly ground pepper to taste

Cook cabbage in a large covered saucepan in a small amount of water just until crisp-tender. Drain and set aside. In a small saucepan melt butter. Add flour and cook 3 minutes over medium heat, stirring constantly. Add milk and chicken broth. Bring to a boil, stirring constantly until mixture thickens. Add dry mustard, white pepper, and thyme. Add salt and pepper to taste. Combine sauce with cooked cabbage. Place in serving bowl and keep in warm oven until ready to serve. Add extra pepper if desired.

Serves 6

Nutrition Information per serving:
Calories: 65 – Fat: 2 gm. – Protein: 3 gm.
Carbohydrate: 9 gm. – Cholesterol: 5 mg. – Fiber: low

Curried Green Beans and Potatoes

 Curry, cumin, and ginger give ordinary beans and potatoes an exotic flavor.

12 small red potatoes

1 pound fresh green beans

1 tablespoon butter or margarine

2 cloves garlic, minced

1 teaspoon curry powder

1 teaspoon salt

1/4 teaspoon cumin

1/4 teaspoon ginger

1/4 teaspoon freshly ground black pepper

1 cup fat-free sour cream

1/4 cup fresh parsley, minced

In a large saucepan, cover potatoes with water and bring to a boil. Cook for 15 minutes. Add fresh green beans. Cover and cook until potatoes and beans are tender. Drain. Quarter potatoes. Set potatoes and beans aside. In a large skillet, melt butter. Add garlic, curry powder, salt, cumin, ginger, and pepper. Cook over medium heat for 1 minute. Reduce heat to low. Add sour cream and stir just until heated through. Do not boil. Add potatoes and beans. Stir gently to mix. Garnish with minced parsley.

Serves 6

Nutrition Information per serving:
Calories: 210 – Fat: 2 gm. – Protein: 6 gm.
Carbohydrate: 42 gm. – Cholesterol: 10 mg. – Fiber: high

German Red Cabbage

 An old recipe from the north woods of Wisconsin.

1 teaspoon dry mustard

1/4 cup cool water

8 cups shredded red cabbage

1 large apple, cored and diced

4 slices bacon, diced

1 tablespoon bacon drippings

1/3 cup brown sugar

1/3 cup cider vinegar

1 teaspoon salt

1/2 teaspoon black pepper

1 teaspoon caraway seed, optional

Preheat oven to 350°. In a small custard cup combine dry mustard with water and set aside. Place shredded cabbage and diced apple in 3-quart baking dish and set aside. In a small skillet fry bacon until crisp. Discard all but 1 tablespoon of the bacon drippings. To the skillet add brown sugar, vinegar, salt, pepper, caraway seeds, and reserved mustard paste. Stir until smooth; pour over shredded cabbage. Stir until well mixed. Cover dish and bake for 30 minutes or until cabbage is tender. Stir to mix well before serving.

Note: It is best to use a cooking variety of apple such as Cortland or Macintosh.

Serves 4

Nutrition Information per serving:
Calories: 180 – Fat: 7 gm. – Protein: 4 gm.
Carbohydrate: 26 gm. – Cholesterol: 10 mg. – Fiber: high

Ginger Glazed Carrots

 So simple but so good with the ginger and allspice.

1 pound baby carrots

1/4 cup water

1 tablespoon butter or margarine

1 tablespoon brown sugar

2 teaspoons orange zest

1/4 teaspoon ground ginger

1/4 teaspoon ground allspice

1/4 teaspoon salt

In a medium saucepan, cook carrots in water until tender. Drain. Add butter, sugar, orange zest, ginger, allspice, and salt to pan with carrots. Stir over medium heat for 1 minute.

Serves 4

Nutrition Information per serving:
Calories: 80 – Fat: 3 gm. – Protein: 1 gm.
Carbohydrate: 12 gm. – Cholesterol: 10 mg. – Fiber: low

Grilled Mushrooms

 A variety of seasonings can be added to mushrooms.
Choose the combination that will complement your meal.

1 pound fresh mushrooms, sliced

2 tablespoons olive oil

1/4 teaspoon paprika

1/4 teaspoon cayenne pepper

1/2 teaspoon salt

1 tablespoon basil or oregano or
   herbs of your choice

Place mushrooms in resealable plastic bag. Add olive oil, paprika, cayenne pepper, salt, and other seasonings of your choice. Mix gently. Refrigerate until ready to use.

When ready to serve, place mushrooms in a vegetable grilling basket and grill over medium heat until tender. Mushrooms may also be cooked in a skillet on the stove over medium heat.

Note: Boiled potatoes that are cut into chunks may be added to the mushrooms before grilling or cooking.

Serves 4

Nutrition Information per serving:
Calories: 90 – Fat: 7 gm. – Protein: 2 gm.
Carbohydrate: 5 – Cholesterol: 0 mg. – Fiber: low

Make-Ahead Mashed Potatoes

These potatoes are wonderful. Even when made days ahead of time, the potatoes taste like you just made them. Good to keep on hand in the refrigerator for a quick warming whenever you are in the mood for great mashed potatoes. The white pepper is an essential ingredient.

5 large russet potatoes, peeled and quartered

1/2 cup fat-free milk

1/2 cup fat-free sour cream

3 ounces fat-free cream cheese

1/4 teaspoon white pepper

salt to taste

Boil potatoes in large saucepan until tender. Drain. In a large bowl, mash potatoes using an electric mixer. Mix in milk and beat until fluffy. Beat in remaining ingredients. Add extra milk if needed for a smooth, light consistency. Transfer potatoes to a lightly buttered casserole dish. Cover and refrigerate.

On the day of serving, heat potatoes in 350° oven until hot, about 30 minutes. They can also be reheated in a microwave.

Serves 5

Nutrition Information per serving:
Calories: 110 – Fat: 0 gm. – Protein: 6 gm.
Carbohydrate: 21 gm. – Cholesterol: 5 mg. – Fiber: low

Orange Pineapple Yams

 *Sweet nutrition.*

3 large yams or sweet potatoes, peeled
    and quartered

2 tablespoons butter or margarine

9 ounces crushed pineapple, drained

1 teaspoon orange rind

2 tablespoons orange juice

1 teaspoon allspice

3/4 teaspoon salt

2 tablespoons brown sugar

1/4 cup flaked coconut

Preheat oven to 350°. In a large saucepan, cook potatoes in boiling water until fork tender. Drain. In a large bowl, mash potatoes and stir in butter, crushed pineapple, orange rind, orange juice, and salt. Spoon into greased 1-quart baking dish. Sprinkle with brown sugar and coconut. Bake covered for 30 minutes.

Serves 6

Nutrition Information per serving:
Calories: 130 – Fat: 4 gm. – Protein: 1 gm.
Carbohydrate: 22 gm. – Cholesterol: 20 mg. – Fiber: low

Sweet Potatoes and Cranberries

 This is a real taste treat and it is beautiful too!
Tangy, yet sweet, and full of good nutrition.

1 1/2 pounds sweet potatoes, cooked
    or canned

1 1/2 cups raw cranberries

1/3 cup brown sugar

1/2 cup uncooked oatmeal

1/4 cup orange juice

1/4 cup butter or margarine, melted

1/2 teaspoon freshly grated nutmeg

Preheat oven to 350°. Grease a 1-quart casserole. Cut the cooked sweet potatoes into slices. Layer sweet potato slices in the casserole. Layer raw cranberries over potatoes. Sprinkle brown sugar on top. Spoon oatmeal over potatoes and cranberries. Combine orange juice and melted butter. Pour over oatmeal. Sprinkle with nutmeg. Cover loosely, and bake for 30 minutes or until cranberries have popped and are tender.

Serves 8

Nutrition Information per serving:
Calories: 170 – Fat: 6 gm. – Protein: 2 gm.
Carbohydrate: 27 gm. – Cholesterol: 15 mg. – Fiber: medium

Side Dishes

Corn and Red Pepper Relish

 This is one of those side dishes you can make ahead and it can spark up your meals for weeks. The turmeric gives it that rich yellow color and the mustard powder gives it the zippy taste.

4 cups frozen corn

1 medium red pepper, chopped

1 medium green pepper, chopped (optional)

1 small onion, chopped

1 stalk celery, chopped

1/2 cup orange juice

1 cup cider vinegar

1/4 cup sugar

1 teaspoon cornstarch

1 teaspoon dry mustard

1 teaspoon salt

1/4 teaspoon white pepper

1/2 teaspoon turmeric

Combine all ingredients in a large saucepan. Bring to a boil, stirring constantly. Reduce heat and simmer uncovered for 15 minutes. Store in covered jars in refrigerator for up to 4 weeks.

Serves 8

Nutrition Information per serving:
Calories: 120 – Fat: 0 gm. – Protein: 3 gm.
Carbohydrate: 28 – Cholesterol: 0 mg. – Fiber: medium

German Potato Salad

 An old traditional recipe but lower in fat with the same good flavor.

4 pounds potatoes (about 8 medium
    potatoes)

6 slices bacon

1 large onion, chopped

2 tablespoons flour

2 cups water

1/3 cup cider vinegar

1/4 cup sugar

1 teaspoon dry mustard

1 teaspoon salt

1/2 teaspoon pepper

1 teaspoon dill weed, optional

In a large saucepan boil potatoes until barely tender. Drain well. Peel and cut into slices. Place in large bowl and set aside. While potatoes are cooking, fry bacon until very crisp in a medium skillet. Remove bacon slices; crumble and set aside. Discard all but 2 tablespoons bacon fat. Add onions to the skillet and cook over medium heat until onions are translucent. Add flour to the pan and cook, stirring constantly, for 3 minutes. Add water, vinegar, sugar, dry mustard, salt, pepper, and dill weed. Bring to a boil and stir until mixture thickens. Combine dressing and potatoes. Gently toss until well coated. Serve warm or at room temperature. Keeps well for a week in the refrigerator.

Serves 6

Nutrition Information per serving:
Calories: 270 – Fat: 3 gm. – Protein: 7 gm.
Carbohydrate: 54 gm. – Cholesterol: 5 mg. – Fiber: high

Herb Basmati Rice

 This will add zest to your rice.

1 tablespoon butter or margarine

1 clove garlic, minced

1 cup basmati rice

2 cups low-fat chicken broth

1/4 teaspoon thyme

1/4 teaspoon rosemary, crushed

4 green onions, finely chopped

2 tablespoons finely chopped fresh basil

2 tablespoons grated Parmesan cheese

In a medium saucepan melt butter. Add garlic and cook 1 minute over low heat. Add rice, broth, thyme, and rosemary. Bring to a boil. Reduce heat, cover, and simmer 20 minutes or until liquid is absorbed. Stir in green onions and fresh basil. When ready to serve top with cheese.

Serves 4

Nutrition Information per serving:
Calories: 290 – Fat: 4 gm. – Protein: 13 gm.
Carbohydrate: 50 gm. – Cholesterol: 10 mg. – Fiber: medium

Jalapeño Rice

 Make it as hot as you like it with chile peppers and cumin.

1 1/2 cups long-grain rice

3 cups low-fat chicken broth

1 tablespoon butter or margarine

1 medium onion, finely chopped

1 small jalapeño chile pepper, seeded
   and minced

1/2 teaspoon oregano

1 teaspoon cumin

1 clove garlic, minced

salt and pepper to taste

In a large saucepan combine rice and chicken broth. Bring to boil. Reduce
heat, cover, and simmer for 20 minutes or until liquid is absorbed.
Meanwhile in a small skillet, melt butter. Add onion, chile pepper, oregano,
and cumin. Cook until onions until translucent. Add garlic and cook 1
minute. Combine onion mixture with cooked rice. Add salt and pepper to
taste.

Serves 4

Nutrition Information per serving:
Calories: 325 – Fat: 3 gm. – Protein: 14 gm.
Carbohydrate: 60 gm. – Cholesterol: 10 mg. – Fiber: low

Lemon and Dill Linguine

 This is an easy way to serve a special side dish. The lemon and dill create a clean refreshing taste that will complement fish, poultry, or fish.

8 ounces linguine

1 tablespoon butter or margarine

2 cloves garlic, finely minced

1/2 cup skim milk

2 teaspoons cornstarch

1 tablespoon lemon juice

1 teaspoon lemon zest

2 tablespoons white wine

1 teaspoon dill weed

1/8 teaspoon nutmeg

1/4 teaspoon white pepper

2 tablespoons minced fresh parsley

salt to taste

1/4 cup freshly grated Romano or
    Parmesan cheese

freshly ground pepper to taste

In a large saucepan cook linguine until just tender. Drain. While linguine is cooking, heat butter in a small skillet. Add garlic and cook over low heat for 2 minutes. In a small custard cup mix milk with cornstarch. Add to skillet and cook, stirring constantly, over medium heat until mixture boils and thickens. Add lemon juice, lemon zest, wine, dill weed, nutmeg, white pepper, parsley, and salt. Add extra wine if mixture is too thick. Taste and adjust seasoning with extra salt and pepper if desired. In a large bowl combine linguine with the sauce. Toss until well mixed. Serve with freshly grated Romano cheese and pepper to taste.

Serves 6

Nutrition Information per serving:
Calories: 190 – Fat: 4 gm. – Protein: 7 gm.
Carbohydrate: 31 gm. – Cholesterol: 10 mg. – Fiber: low

Mexican Lentils

 A spicy addition to your meal or serve as a healthy main course.

1 cup lentils

3 cups low-fat chicken broth or vegetable broth

1 tablespoon olive oil

1 small onion, minced

1 small red bell pepper, chopped

2 cloves garlic, minced

11-ounce can corn

1 tablespoon chili powder

1/2 teaspoon cumin

8 ounces tomato sauce

1 tablespoon red wine vinegar

1–2 teaspoons molasses

salt and freshly ground pepper to taste

In a large saucepan combine lentils and broth. Bring to a boil. Reduce heat, cover, and simmer for 20 to 30 minutes or until lentils are tender. Drain any liquid that was not absorbed. In a small skillet heat oil. Cook onions and red peppers over medium heat until onions are translucent. Add garlic and cook 1 minute. Add corn, chili powder, cumin, tomato sauce, vinegar, and 1 teaspoon molasses. Simmer until heated through and flavors are blended. Taste and add extra molasses if desired. Add salt and pepper to taste.

Serves 6

Nutrition Information per serving:
Calories: 250 – Fat: 3 gm. – Protein: 17 gm.
Carbohydrate: 40 – Cholesterol: 0 mg. – Fiber: very high

Orange Rice with Dried Cranberries and Apples

The cranberries and apples with allspice complement pork or chicken meals.

2 cups brown rice

4 cups low-fat chicken broth

1/2 cup dried cranberries

1 large apple, cored and diced

2 tablespoons minced fresh parsley

1 tablespoon orange zest

2 tablespoons orange juice

1/4 teaspoon allspice

salt and pepper to taste

Preheat oven to 350°. Butter a 2-quart casserole dish. In a medium heavy saucepan, combine rice and chicken broth. Bring to a boil. Reduce heat, cover, and simmer for 35 to 40 minutes or until liquid is absorbed. Remove from heat. Add dried cranberries, apples, parsley, orange zest, orange juice, and allspice. Mix well. Add salt and pepper to taste. Spoon into buttered casserole dish. Bake for 20 minutes or until heated thoroughly and apples are tender.

Serves 6

Nutrition Information per serving:
Calories: 285 – Fat: 2 gm. – Protein: 12 gm.
Carbohydrate: 55 – Cholesterol: 0 mg. – Fiber: medium

Orzo with Peppers and Peas

 Add other vegetables of your choice but be sure to use freshly ground pepper.

1 tablespoon butter or margarine

1 medium onion, minced

1 medium leek, thinly sliced, white part
   only (optional)

1 clove garlic, minced

1 medium red bell pepper, thinly sliced

2 cups low-fat chicken broth

1 cup uncooked orzo

1 cup frozen green peas

salt to taste

freshly ground pepper to taste

1/2 cup grated Parmesan cheese

2 tablespoons minced fresh parsley

In a large skillet melt butter. Add onion and leek. Cook over medium heat until onions are translucent. Add garlic and red pepper. Cook 2 minutes. Add chicken broth and orzo. Bring to a boil. Reduce heat and simmer 10 minutes. Add peas and cook 2 minutes or until peas are done. Add salt and pepper to taste. When ready to serve top with cheese and garnish with parsley.

Serves 4

Nutrition Information per serving:
Calories: 220 – Fat: 6 gm. – Protein: 15 gm.
Carbohydrate: 27 gm. – Cholesterol: 15 mg. – Fiber: high

Saffron Rice

 Saffron will give this rice a light golden yellow color and a fragrant, rich flavor.

2 tablespoons butter or margarine

1 small onion, finely chopped

1 1/2 cups long-grain white rice

1 medium pinch saffron threads, crumbled
   (about 35 threads)

3 cups low-fat chicken broth

salt to taste

In a medium skillet melt butter. Add onions, and cook until translucent. Add rice and fry over medium heat, stirring constantly, until rice is lightly browned. Add saffron and chicken broth. Bring to a boil. Reduce heat, cover, and simmer for 20 minutes or until rice is tender and liquid is absorbed. Add salt to taste.

Serves 4

Nutrition Information per serving:
Calories: 275 – Fat: 5 gm. – Protein: 9 gm.
Carbohydrate: 48 gm. – Cholesterol: 15 mg. – Fiber: low

Spaetzle

 Surprise yourself and your family with a homemade dish from the past. The white pepper, nutmeg, and fresh parsley are essential ingredients.

2 cups flour

3 eggs

1 teaspoon salt

1/2 teaspoon white pepper

1/4 teaspoon nutmeg

1/4 cup minced fresh parsley, divided

3/4 cup milk

2 tablespoons butter

1/2 cup seasoned bread crumbs

In a medium bowl, mix flour, eggs, salt, pepper, nutmeg, 1 tablespoon minced parsley, and enough milk to make a heavy dough. Drop very small pieces of dough into a pan of boiling water. Cook for about 5 minutes or until dough is completely cooked. Stir occasionally. Remove spaetzle with a large strainer spoon and place in a colander. Rinse with cold water; drain well. Melt butter in a nonstick skillet. Add the cooked spaetzle and sauté in butter over medium heat until golden brown. Add bread crumbs and brown lightly. Sprinkle with remaining parsley. Serve as a side dish with meat or other German dishes.

Serves 6

Nutrition Information per serving:
Calories: 260 – Fat: 6 gm. – Protein: 10 gm.
Carbohydrate: 42 gm. – Cholesterol: 100 mg. – Fiber: low

Wild Rice Pilaf with Hazelnuts and Dried Cranberries

 The color is beautiful and the flavor is subtle.

1 cup wild rice

1/2 teaspoon rosemary, crushed

4 cups low-fat chicken broth, divided

1/2 cup white rice

3/4 cup dried apricots, diced

3/4 cup dried cranberries

3/4 cup hazelnuts, toasted

1/4 cup fresh chopped parsley

1/2 teaspoon allspice

1 tablespoon butter or margarine, melted

salt and pepper to taste

In a large saucepan combine wild rice and rosemary in 3 cups chicken broth. Bring to a boil; cover, reduce heat, and simmer for 45 minutes or until rice is tender. Do not overcook. Drain off any excess liquid. In a small saucepan cook white rice and dried apricots in 1 cup chicken broth for 20 minutes or until rice is tender and has absorbed the broth. In a 1 1/2 quart casserole dish combine wild rice, white rice, dried cranberries, hazelnuts, parsley, allspice, and butter. Add salt and pepper to taste. Reheat in microwave just before serving.

Note: Pecans can be substituted for the hazelnuts.

Serves 6

Nutrition Information per serving:
Calories: 300 – Fat: 6 gm. – Protein: 14 gm.
Carbohydrate: 48 gm. – Cholesterol: 5 mg. – Fiber: high

Wild Rice with Mushrooms

 Wild rice can be prepared ahead of time and refrigerated until ready to use. Rosemary, thyme, and cayenne pepper add the interesting flavor.

1/2 cup wild rice	1/8 teaspoon cayenne pepper
1 1/2 cups low-fat chicken broth	1 pound fresh mushrooms, sliced
2 tablespoons butter or margarine	1/3 cup dry sherry
1/2 teaspoon dried rosemary	salt and freshly ground pepper to taste
1/4 teaspoon thyme	

Wash wild rice in cold water. In a medium saucepan combine rice and chicken broth. Bring to a boil. Reduce heat, cover, and simmer about 1 hour or until liquid is absorbed and rice is tender. Remove from heat. While rice is cooking, melt butter in a large nonstick skillet. Add rosemary, thyme, pepper, and mushrooms. Cook over medium heat about 10 minutes until mushrooms are tender. Add sherry and cook until liquid is reduced by about half. Season to taste with salt and pepper. Add rice and stir until well mixed and rice is heated through.

Note: A wild rice and white rice mixture may be used in place of all wild rice.

Serves 4

Nutrition Information per serving:
Calories: 175 – Fat: 6 gm. – Protein: 9 gm.
Carbohydrate: 21 gm. – Cholesterol: 15 mg. – Fiber: medium

Soups and Stews

Beef and Bean Cassoulet

 Cassoulet is pronounced ka-soo-LAY. *The ingredients can be changed to suit your taste or to use the meat and vegetables you have on hand. Make enough to warm up for leftovers.*

2 pounds lean beef roast	3 cups water
1/2 cup flour	2 1/2 cups red wine, divided
1 teaspoon paprika	2 bay leaves
1 teaspoon salt	4 large carrots, peeled and sliced
1/2 teaspoon black pepper	16 small red potatoes, unpeeled
2 tablespoons corn oil	15-ounce can white beans
2 large onions, cubed	salt and freshly ground pepper to taste

Cut beef roast into 2-inch cubes. In a gallon plastic bag, combine flour, paprika, salt, and pepper. Add meat cubes and toss until well coated. In a large heavy pan, heat corn oil. Over medium-hot heat, brown beef cubes, stirring occasionally. Add onions and cook until onions are translucent. Add water, 2 cups wine, and bay leaves. Bring to a boil, stirring to deglaze pan. Add carrots and potatoes. Cover pan and simmer over low heat for 1–2 hours or until meat and vegetables are tender. Check occasionally and add water if it gets too dry. Add canned beans and 1/2 cup wine. Cook 10 more minutes or until heated thoroughly. Add salt and pepper to taste. Serve in large shallow soup bowls.

Note: The cassoulet may be placed in 325° oven for 1 1/2 hours instead of cooking on top of the stove. Check occasionally and add water if it gets too dry.

Serves 8

Nutrition Information per serving:
Calories: 420 – Fat: 9 gm. – Protein: 33 gm.
Carbohydrate: 50 gm. – Cholesterol: 65 mg. – Fiber: high

Beef Vegetable Soup

 Home sweet home with a big pot of healthy soup. The flavors of the meat and vegetables are enhanced by the thyme, oregano, and bay leaves.

2 pounds lean beef roast, cut into 1/2-inch pieces

1 tablespoon vegetable oil

1 large onions, chopped

6 cups (48 ounces) canned low-fat beef broth

30-ounce can tomatoes

1 teaspoon thyme

1/2 teaspoon oregano

1/2 teaspoon basil

2 bay leaves

1 teaspoon freshly ground pepper

2 large carrots, peeled and diced

1 cup frozen green beans

1/2 cup pasta shells

1 cup frozen corn

1 cup frozen peas

salt to taste

freshly ground pepper to taste

1–3 teaspoons sugar, optional

In a large heavy soup pot, heat oil and brown beef cubes over medium-hot heat. Add onions and cook until translucent. Add beef broth, canned tomatoes, thyme, oregano, basil, bay leaves, and pepper. Bring to a boil. Reduce heat; cover and simmer for 1 to 2 hours or until meat is very tender. Add carrots, green beans, and pasta shells. Boil gently until vegetables and pasta are tender. Add additional beef broth or water to thin the soup to desired consistency. Add corn and peas. Boil 3 to 5 more minutes. Remove bay leaves before serving. Adjust seasoning with salt and pepper. If soup is slightly bitter add a small amount of sugar.

Serves 10

Nutrition Information per serving:
Calories: 295 – Fat: 15 gm. – Protein: 22 gm.
Carbohydrate: 18 gm. – Cholesterol: 55 mg. – Fiber: high

Broccoli Cheese Soup

 This is a delicious low-fat version of a soup that is usually loaded with calories and fat. The spices make the difference.

2 tablespoons butter or margarine

1 medium onion, finely chopped

1/4 pound fresh mushrooms, sliced

2 cloves garlic, minced

2 tablespoons flour

1 cup low-fat chicken broth

11 ounces fat-free half-and-half

1/4 teaspoon thyme

1/4 teaspoon white pepper

10 ounces frozen chopped broccoli
(about 3 cups)

3 ounces fat-free processed American cheese

salt and pepper to taste

In a large heavy saucepan heat butter. Add onions and cook over medium heat until translucent. Add mushrooms and garlic and cook until mushrooms are tender. Add flour and stir over medium heat for 2 minutes. Add broth, half-and-half, thyme, and white pepper. Bring to a boil, stirring constantly until mixture thickens slightly. Add broccoli, and cook just until broccoli is tender. Add cheese and stir until cheese melts. Add salt and pepper to taste. If soup is too thick add extra chicken broth to thin.

Serves 4

Nutrition Information per serving:
Calories: 200 – Fat: 6 gm. – Protein: 18 gm.
Carbohydrate: 19 gm. – Cholesterol: 20 mg. – Fiber: medium

Crab Potato Soup

 Super, elegant flavor with sherry and a combination of peppers.

3 tablespoons butter or margarine

1 medium onion, chopped

1/2 cup diced celery

3 tablespoons flour

3 cups chicken stock

2 cups fat-free milk

1/2 teaspoon dry mustard

2 teaspoons Worcestershire sauce

1/4 teaspoon cayenne pepper

1/4 teaspoon white pepper

3 medium potatoes, peeled and diced

1/2 pound crab surimi seafood chunks

1/4 cup sherry

salt to taste

freshly ground pepper to taste

In heavy pan, cook onions and celery in butter over low heat until onions are translucent. Stir in flour and cook for 3 minutes, stirring constantly. Add stock and milk. Bring to a boil, stirring continually until mixture thickens. Reduce heat. Add dry mustard, Worcestershire sauce, cayenne pepper, white pepper, and potatoes. Simmer about 30 minutes or until potatoes are tender. Add crab and simmer another 10 minutes. Add sherry just before serving and adjust seasoning with salt and freshly ground pepper.

Serves 6

Nutrition Information per serving:
Calories: 185 – Fat: 7 gm. – Protein: 11 gm.
Carbohydrate: 20 gm. – Cholesterol: 30 mg. – Fiber: low

Easy Chili

 Great chili—just as good as long, complicated recipes, yet it is ready in less than an hour. This tastes even better the next day.

1 pound extra lean ground beef	1 cup water
1 large onion, chopped	30-ounce can kidney beans
1/2 teaspoon salt	1 tablespoon chili powder
1/2 teaspoon pepper	1 teaspoon cumin
15-ounce can peeled, diced tomatoes	1/2 teaspoon oregano
15-ounce can tomato sauce	2 fresh jalapeño chiles, minced (optional)

In a large, heavy, nonstick pan, brown meat and onion. Drain well. Season with salt and pepper. Add tomatoes, tomato sauce, water, kidney beans, chili powder, cumin, oregano, and chiles. Bring to a boil. Reduce heat and simmer uncovered for about 30 minutes.

Note: For a thinner chili, substitute a 49-ounce can of tomato juice for the 15-ounce can of tomatoes and 8-ounce can of tomato sauce.

Serves 6

Nutrition Information per serving:
Calories: 330 – Fat: 14 gm. – Protein: 23 gm.
Carbohydrate: 28 gm. – Cholesterol: 50 mg. – Fiber: low

Egg Drop Soup

 A light appetizer soup seasoned with ginger and a dash of cayenne pepper.

6 cups (48 ounces) low-fat chicken broth

1 cup diced cooked chicken

4 green onions, finely chopped

1 teaspoon minced fresh ginger or
    1/4 teaspoon ground ginger

1 tablespoon soy sauce

1 tablespoon rice vinegar

1 tablespoon dry sherry

1/8 teaspoon cayenne pepper

2 tablespoons cornstarch

1/4 cup cold water

2 eggs, lightly beaten

Heat chicken broth in a large saucepan. Add chicken, onions, ginger, soy sauce, vinegar, sherry, and pepper. Bring to a boil. In a small custard cup mix cornstarch with water. Pour into boiling soup, and stir constantly until soup thickens slightly. Pour beaten eggs into boiling mixture, stirring to coagulate strings of egg. (Soup must be boiling when adding egg.)

Serves 6

Nutrition Information per serving:
Calories: 120 – Fat: 3 gm. – Protein: 13 gm.
Carbohydrate: 10 gm. – Cholesterol: 80 mg. – Fiber: low

French Onion Soup

 The port wine, fresh pepper, and thyme provide a rich, slightly sweet flavor.

1 tablespoon olive oil	1/2 teaspoon freshly ground pepper
2 jumbo sweet onions, thinly sliced	1/2 cup port wine
1 tablespoon brown sugar	salt to taste
2 tablespoons flour	4 slices French bread
6 cups (48 ounces) fat-free beef broth	4 ounces Swiss cheese, grated
1/2 teaspoon ground thyme	

In a large, heavy saucepan, heat olive oil. Add onions and sugar. Cook over medium heat for 15 to 20 minutes or until onions are very tender. Stir occasionally and turn heat to low if mixture is browning. In a shaker, mix flour with 1 cup of the beef broth. Shake until smooth and pour into pan with onions. Add remaining beef broth, thyme, and pepper. Bring to a boil, and stir occasionally. Reduce heat and simmer for at least 30 minutes. Add wine. Adjust seasoning with salt and extra pepper if desired. When ready to serve, heat oven broiler. Spoon soup into individual ovenproof bowls. Top with slice of French bread and grated cheese. Place under oven broiler until cheese is melted.

Serves 4

Nutrition Information per serving:
Calories: 250 – Fat: 5 gm. – Protein: 27 gm.
Carbohydrate: 24 gm. – Cholesterol: 10 mg. – Fiber: low

Great Northern Bean Soup

 A hearty meal made fast and easy with canned beans.

1 tablespoon olive oil	30-ounce can Great Northern beans, drained
1 large onion, chopped	3/4 pound lean ham, cubed
2 stalks celery, chopped	1 bay leaf
1 cup peeled and chopped carrots	1 teaspoon dried thyme
2 cloves garlic, minced	salt and freshly ground pepper to taste
4 cups low-fat chicken broth	

In a large frying pan, heat oil. Cook onions, celery, and carrots over medium heat until onions are translucent. Add garlic and cook 1 minute. Add chicken broth, beans, ham, bay leaf, and thyme. Simmer 30 to 45 minutes until flavors are blended. Add extra chicken broth if soup gets too thick. Remove bay leaf. Add salt and pepper to taste.

Serves 4

Nutrition Information per serving:
Calories: 360 – Fat: 9 gm. – Protein: 30 gm.
Carbohydrate: 40 gm. – Cholesterol: 35 mg. – Fiber: very high

Hot and Sour Soup

 Make your own special Chinese soup with a unique seasoning combination.

1/2 ounce dried shiitake mushrooms

1 chicken breast without skin

6 cups (48 ounces) low-fat chicken broth

1 cup (8 ounces) canned bamboo shoots

1/4 cup rice vinegar

1 tablespoon sugar

1 tablespoon sherry

1 tablespoon soy sauce

1/2 teaspoon ginger

1 teaspoon sesame oil

1/2 teaspoon white pepper

1/4 cup water

2 tablespoons cornstarch

1 teaspoon dry mustard

1 medium green onion, finely chopped

In a small saucepan combine mushrooms with 2 cups water. Bring to a boil; remove from heat and let stand for 30 minutes. Drain and cut into thin strips. In a large saucepan combine chicken and broth. Bring to a boil; reduce heat and simmer for 20 minutes or until chicken is done. Remove chicken and cut into small pieces. Return chicken to the broth. Add bamboo shoots, vinegar, sugar, sherry, soy sauce, ginger, sesame oil, and pepper. In a small custard cup mix water, cornstarch, and dry mustard until smooth. Add to the soup, and stir constantly until soup boils and thickens slightly. Serve in warm bowls and top with green onions.

Serves 6

Nutrition Information per serving:
Calories: 75 – Fat: 1 gm. – Protein: 7 gm.
Carbohydrate: 10 gm. – Cholesterol: 10 mg. – Fiber: medium

Mexican Pork Chili

 Make it as hot as you like with chili powder and cumin.

1 1/2 pounds boneless pork loin, trimmed
  of visible fat
1/2 teaspoon salt
1/2 teaspoon black pepper
1 tablespoon cooking oil
1 large onion, chopped
2 cloves garlic, minced
2 teaspoons chili powder
1/2 teaspoon cumin

1/4 teaspoon cinnamon
30-ounce can diced tomatoes with garlic
  and onion
30-ounce can kidney beans
1 1/2 cups low-fat chicken broth
dash or more Tabasco, to taste
2 green onions, chopped
1/2 cup shredded mozzarella cheese

Cut pork loin into 1/2-inch cubes. Sprinkle with salt and pepper. In a large, heavy saucepan heat oil over medium-hot heat. Add pork and brown on all sides. Reduce heat to medium. Add onions and cook until translucent. Add garlic and cook 1 minute. Add chili powder, cumin, cinnamon, undrained tomatoes, undrained kidney beans, and chicken broth. Bring to a boil. Reduce heat, cover, and simmer for 30 minutes. Adjust seasoning with extra salt and pepper, and Tabasco if desired. Uncover and cook until the desired thickness. Serve in warm bowls. Top with green onions and cheese.

Serves 8

Nutrition Information per serving:
Calories: 280 – Fat: 8 gm. – Protein: 29 gm.
Carbohydrate: 23 gm. – Cholesterol: 50 mg. – Fiber: low

Mushroom and Carrot Soup with Brandy

 A light delicate soup with nutmeg and brandy to warm the heart.

2 tablespoons butter or margarine	4 cups chicken broth, divided
1 large onion, chopped	3 cups fat-free milk
1 clove garlic, minced	1/4 teaspoon white pepper
2 pounds fresh mushrooms, sliced	1/4 teaspoon nutmeg
3/4 cup peeled and finely sliced carrots	2 tablespoons brandy
3 tablespoons flour	salt to taste

In a large saucepan, melt butter. Add onions and cook over medium heat until translucent. Add garlic and cook 1 minute. Add mushrooms and carrots and cook until tender. Combine flour with 1 cup of the chicken broth in a shaker. Add to mushroom mixture. Add remaining broth and bring to a boil, stirring continually until mixture thickens. Add milk, white pepper, and nutmeg. Heat to simmering. Stir in brandy just before serving. Add salt to taste.

Note: For a richer soup, substitute half-and-half for the milk. It will add an extra 60 calories per serving.

Serves 8

Nutrition Information per serving:
Calories: 115 – Fat: 4 gm. – Protein: 7 gm.
Carbohydrate: 13 gm. – Cholesterol: 10 mg. – Fiber: medium

Pasta e Fagioli

 *This traditional pasta and bean soup tastes so good
with just the right mix of Italian seasonings.*

1 tablespoon olive oil

1 medium onion, diced

2 stalks celery, tops removed, sliced

2 large carrots, peeled and sliced

2 cloves garlic, minced

4 cups low-fat chicken broth

1/4 cup red wine

15-ounce can white beans, undrained

15-ounce can red kidney beans, undrained

14-ounce can diced Italian tomatoes

1 bay leaf

1 teaspoon basil

1/2 teaspoon oregano

1 cup dried ditalini or small shell pasta

1/4 cup chopped fresh parsley

salt and freshly ground pepper to taste

1 cup freshly grated Parmesan cheese

In a large soup pot, heat the olive oil. Add onions, celery, and carrots.
Cook over low heat for 5 to 7 minutes. Add garlic and cook an additional 1
minute. Do not brown any of the vegetables. The celery and carrots will
still be firm. Add broth, wine, white beans, kidney beans, tomatoes, bay
leaf, basil, and oregano. Simmer for 10 minutes. Add pasta and parsley and
cook until the pasta is just cooked. Add extra broth if soup is too thick.
Adjust the seasonings with salt and pepper. Remove the bay leaf. Serve in
warmed pasta bowls with a generous amount of freshly grated Parmesan
cheese.

Serves 8

Nutrition Information per serving:
Calories: 235 – Fat: 5 gm. – Protein: 14 gm.
Carbohydrate: 34 gm. – Cholesterol: 10 mg. – Fiber: very high

Pea Soup with Ham

 Warm, soothing soup at any time of the year.
The secret ingredient is the ground coriander.

16 ounces dry green split peas	3 stalks celery, chopped
6 cups (48 ounces) low-fat chicken stock	2 large carrots, peeled and chopped
2 large potatoes, peeled and chopped	1 pound lean ham, diced
1 bay leaf	1/2 teaspoon thyme
1 tablespoon cooking oil	salt and pepper to taste
1 large onion, chopped	1/2 teaspoon ground coriander

Wash peas in a colander. Place in large cooking pot and add water to cover at least 3 to 4 inches above peas. Bring to a boil; remove from heat and let sit for about an hour. Drain off water. Add chicken stock, potatoes, and bay leaf to the pot. Bring to a boil and simmer uncovered for 1 to 2 hours until peas are tender and mushy. Stir occasionally. (Do not add any salt, salty foods, or high-acid foods before the peas are soft because salt and acid ingredients will prevent the peas from becoming soft.) While peas are cooking, heat oil in a medium skillet. Cook onions, celery, and carrots over medium heat until onions are translucent. Remove from heat and set aside. After peas are soft, add onions, celery, carrots, ham, and thyme. Simmer for 20 to 30 minutes or until vegetables are tender and soup has thickened. Stir occasionally and add extra water or chicken broth if soup gets too thick. Adjust seasoning with salt and pepper. Remove bay leaf. Sprinkle each serving with ground coriander.

Optional: For a very smooth consistency, process soup in a food processor or blender.

Serves 8

Nutrition Information per serving:
Calories: 310 – Fat: 4 gm. – Protein: 27 gm.
Carbohydrate: 42 gm. – Cholesterol: 25 mg. – Fiber: high

Portuguese Bean Soup

 The combination of beans, potatoes, carrots, cabbage, and kielbasa makes a memorable meal. This can also be cooked slowly all day in a Crockpot.

1 tablespoon olive oil

1 large onion, chopped

3 cloves garlic, minced

6 cups chicken stock

1/2 pound low-fat kielbasa, diced

4 medium potatoes, peeled and diced

2 large carrots, peeled and chopped

28-ounce can tomatoes

3 cups shredded cabbage

30-ounce can kidney beans

1 teaspoon paprika

1/2 teaspoon thyme

1/2 teaspoon cayenne pepper

salt and freshly ground pepper to taste

In a large soup pan, heat olive oil. Add onion and cook over medium heat until translucent. Add garlic and cook 1 minute. Add all remaining ingredients. Bring to a boil. Reduce heat and simmer for 1 to 2 hours, stirring occasionally. Cook until vegetables are tender and soup has thickened slightly. Adjust seasoning with salt and pepper.

Serves 8

Nutrition Information per serving:
Calories: 275 – Fat: 9 gm. – Protein: 15 gm.
Carbohydrate: 33 gm. – Cholesterol: 20 mg. – Fiber: medium

Potato Mushroom Soup

 Dill weed and white pepper add just the right touch.

2 tablespoons butter or margarine

2 medium leeks (white part only), chopped

1/2 pound fresh mushrooms, sliced

2 large carrots, chopped

6 cups chicken stock

1/2 teaspoon dill weed

1/2 teaspoon white pepper

1 bay leaf

1 teaspoon salt

5 medium potatoes, peeled and diced

1 cup fat-free milk

2 tablespoons flour

freshly ground pepper to taste

In a large stockpot, melt butter. Over medium heat cook leeks for 3 to 4 minutes or until tender. Add mushrooms and cook until mushrooms are soft. Add carrots, chicken stock, dill weed, white pepper, bay leaf, salt, and potatoes. Bring to a boil. Reduce heat and simmer for about 1 hour or until potatoes are very tender. Mix milk and flour in a shaker. Pour into soup, stirring constantly. Bring to a boil and cook 2 minutes, until soup thickens slightly. Add additional salt and pepper to taste. Remove bay leaf. Garnish with sprinkles of dill weed.

Serves 6

Nutrition Information per serving:
Calories: 200 – Fat: 6 gm. – Protein: 10 gm.
Carbohydrate: 26 gm. – Cholesterol: 15 mg. – Fiber: medium

Seafood Chowder

 The thyme, oregano, and white pepper provide the good flavor.

1 tablespoon butter or margarine

1 large onion, chopped

2 stalks celery, chopped

2 cups chicken broth

2 large carrots, peeled and diced

2 large potatoes, peeled and diced

1 large bay leaf

1/4 teaspoon thyme

1/4 teaspoon oregano

1/2 teaspoon white pepper

2 cups fat-free milk, divided

3 tablespoons flour

1 pound cod, cut in 1-inch cubes

1/2 teaspoon salt

freshly ground pepper to taste

fresh parsley for garnish

In a large saucepan melt butter. Add onion and celery and cook over medium heat until onions are translucent. Add broth, carrots, potatoes, bay leaf, thyme, oregano, and white pepper. Bring to a boil. Reduce heat and simmer until vegetables are tender. In a shaker mix 1 cup of the milk with the flour. Add milk-flour mixture and remaining milk to the pan. Bring to a boil, stirring constantly. Boil gently for 2 minutes or until soup thickens slightly. Reduce heat and add cod. Cook over low heat until fish is thoroughly cooked. Add salt and pepper to taste. Garnish with parsley.

Serves 4

Nutrition Information per serving:
Calories: 250 – Fat: 5 gm. – Protein: 28 gm.
Carbohydrate: 24 gm. – Cholesterol: 60 mg. – Fiber: low

Spicy Lentil Soup

 Lentils by themselves have very little flavor, but the addition of some surprise spices makes this a soup to remember.

1 tablespoon olive oil	1 cup lentils, washed
1 large onion, diced	4 cups chicken stock
2 stalks celery, diced	2 medium tomatoes, seeded and chopped
2 cloves garlic, finely minced	1/2 cup grated carrots
1/4 teaspoon cinnamon	1 teaspoon lemon juice, optional
1/2–1 teaspoon ground cumin	salt to taste
1/4 teaspoon ground cloves	freshly ground pepper to taste

In a large, heavy saucepan, heat oil. Cook onions and celery until onions are translucent. Reduce heat and add garlic, cinnamon, cumin, and cloves. Cook for 1 minute. Add lentils and chicken stock. Bring to a boil; reduce heat, cover, and simmer for 30 to 40 minutes or until lentils are soft. Add tomatoes, carrots, and lemon juice. Cook another 20 minutes until carrots are tender. Add additional chicken stock to thin if desired. Season with salt and freshly ground pepper.

Serves 6

Nutrition Information per serving:
Calories: 170 – Fat: 3 gm. – Protein: 13 gm.
Carbohydrate: 23 – Cholesterol: 0 mg. – Fiber: very high

Turkey Vegetable Soup

 This is one of those healthy, yet great tasting meals.
Low-fat ground turkey works well in this flavorful soup.

1 tablespoon vegetable oil

1 pound ground turkey white meat

1 medium onion, finely chopped

6 cups (48 ounces) tomato juice

15-ounce can beans

11-ounce can corn

2 medium potatoes, peeled and diced

1/2 cup water

1 teaspoon chili powder

salt and freshly ground pepper to taste

In a large saucepan heat oil. Brown turkey over medium heat. Add onions and cook until translucent. Add tomato juice, undrained beans, undrained corn, potatoes, water, and chili powder. Bring to a boil. Reduce heat and simmer for at least 30 minutes or until potatoes are tender. Add extra chili powder if desired. Add salt and pepper to taste.

Serves 6

Nutrition Information per serving:
Calories: 340 – Fat: 8 gm. – Protein: 24 gm.
Carbohydrate: 43 gm. – Cholesterol: 45 mg. – Fiber: high

White Chili

 Create this unique chili with cumin, oregano, chicken, and white beans.

1 tablespoon olive oil

1 large onion, chopped

2 cloves garlic, minced

3 cups cubed cooked chicken

30-ounce can navy beans or other white
    beans

6 cups (48 ounces) low-fat chicken broth

1 teaspoon cumin

2 teaspoons oregano

salt to taste

freshly ground pepper to taste

1 cup shredded low-fat cheddar cheese

6 tablespoons fat-free sour cream

cayenne pepper, optional

In a large pan heat oil. Cook onions over medium heat until translucent. Add garlic and cook 1 minute. Add chicken, undrained beans, chicken broth, cumin, and oregano. Bring to a boil; reduce heat and simmer for 20 minutes. Add salt and pepper to taste. Serve in warm bowls topped with shredded cheese and a dollop of sour cream. For a hotter chili, add cayenne pepper to suit your taste.

Serves 6

Nutrition Information per serving:
Calories: 370 – Fat: 8 gm. – Protein: 40 gm.
Carbohydrate: 34 gm. – Cholesterol: 65 mg. – Fiber: very high

Wild Rice Soup

 *Delicate and elegant.*

1 small onion, minced

1 tablespoon butter or margarine

2 tablespoons flour

1/2 teaspoon nutmeg

4 cups chicken broth

2 cups cooked wild rice

1/2 cup grated carrots

1 cup fat-free half-and-half

1 tablespoon sherry

salt and freshly ground pepper to taste

1/4 cup slivered almonds, toasted

Cook onions in butter in a heavy saucepan until onions are translucent. Stir in flour and nutmeg. Cook over low heat, stirring constantly, for 3 minutes. Add chicken broth and bring to a boil, stirring continually. Add cooked wild rice and grated carrots. Bring to a boil. Reduce heat and cook for 10 minutes or until carrots are tender. Add half-and-half and heat thoroughly. Add sherry and salt and pepper to taste. Serve with toasted almonds on top.

Serves 6

Nutrition Information per serving:
Calories: 175 – Fat: 6 gm. – Protein: 8 gm.
Carbohydrate: 22 gm. – Cholesterol: 10 mg. – Fiber: low

Winter Squash Soup

 *So full of vitamin A (8,000 I.U. per serving)
with the warm taste of cinnamon and nutmeg.*

4 cups low-fat chicken broth	1/8 teaspoon cinnamon
3 cups cooked squash (1 large acorn squash)	1/8 teaspoon nutmeg
1/4 teaspoon white pepper	1/4 cup dry sherry
1/2 teaspoon marjoram	salt to taste
1 cup evaporated fat-free milk	freshly ground pepper to taste

In a large saucepan, combine chicken broth and cooked squash. Mash with electric mixer. Add white pepper, marjoram, evaporated milk, cinnamon, and nutmeg. Bring to a boil. Reduce heat and simmer 10 to 15 minutes. Add sherry right before serving. Season with salt and pepper to taste.

Note: In place of acorn squash, use 3 cups of any other winter squash such as butternut squash.

Serves 6

Nutrition Information per serving:
Calories: 65 – Fat: 0 gm. – Protein: 5 gm.
Carbohydrate: 11 gm. – Cholesterol: 4 mg. – Fiber: very low

Meatless Meals

Baked Penne Pasta with Mushroom, Olive, and Tomato Sauce

A robust-flavored Italian pasta meal to make ahead for either a family or company meal.

1/2 pound (2 1/2 cups dry) penne pasta	1 teaspoon basil
1 tablespoon olive oil	1/4 teaspoon oregano
1 medium onion, diced	1/2 teaspoon freshly ground pepper
2 cloves garlic, minced	salt to taste
1/2 pound fresh mushrooms, sliced	1/2 teaspoon sugar, optional
15-ounce can Italian tomatoes	10 large black olives, sliced
4 ounces tomato sauce	1/2 cup grated low-fat mozzarella cheese
1/4 cup red wine	1/4 cup grated Parmesan cheese
1 large bay leaf	

Preheat oven to 375°. Grease an 8 x 8 inch baking pan. Cook pasta in a large pan of rapidly boiling water until al dente. Do not overcook. Drain and set aside. Meanwhile, in a large skillet heat oil; add onions. Cook over medium heat until onions are translucent. Add garlic and mushrooms and cook until mushrooms are tender. Add tomatoes, tomato sauce, wine, bay leaf, basil, oregano, and pepper. Partially cover pan and simmer for 15 to 30 minutes. (Preheat oven to 375°.) Add salt to taste. If the sauce is bitter add 1/2 teaspoon of sugar or more as desired. Add olives and adjust seasonings with extra salt and pepper to taste. Remove bay leaf. Reserve 1/2 cup of sauce. Mix remaining sauce with cooked pasta. Spread in baking pan. Top with reserved sauce and lightly press into the pasta. Cover with grated mozzarella and Parmesan cheese. Cover pan with aluminum foil. Bake for 10 minutes. Remove foil and bake for an additional 10 minutes.

Note: This can be made ahead and refrigerated overnight. Increase baking time an extra 10 minutes or bake until heated through.

Serves 4

Nutrition Information per serving:
Calories: 375 – Fat: 10 gm. – Protein: 16 gm.
Carbohydrate: 56 gm. – Cholesterol: 10 mg. – Fiber: high

Broccoli, Mushroom, and Rice Skillet Dinner

 This is so good with the Italian seasoning combination.

1 1/2 cups long-grain rice

3 1/2 cups low-fat chicken or vegetable broth, divided

1 tablespoon cooking oil

1 large onion, chopped

2 cloves garlic, minced

1 pound fresh mushrooms, sliced

1/4 teaspoon thyme

1/2 teaspoon oregano

1/2 teaspoon rosemary, crushed

1/4 teaspoon marjoram

5 cups fresh broccoli florets

1/2 cup minced fresh parsley

1/2 cup walnuts, toasted

1 1/2 cups grated low-fat cheddar cheese or other cheese of your choice

salt to taste

freshly ground pepper to taste

Combine rice and 3 cups broth in medium saucepan. Bring to a boil. Reduce heat, cover, and cook about 45 minutes or until liquid is absorbed. Set aside. In large skillet, heat oil. Cook onions over medium heat until translucent. Add garlic and cook 1 minute. Add mushrooms, thyme, oregano, rosemary, and marjoram. Cook until mushrooms are tender. Add remaining 1/2 cup chicken broth, broccoli, and parsley. Cover pan and cook over medium heat until broccoli is tender-crisp. Stir in cooked rice. Sprinkle with nuts and cheese. Gently mix and heat over low heat until cheese has melted. Add salt and pepper to taste.

Serves 6

Nutrition Information per serving:
Calories: 350 – Fat: 7 gm. – Protein: 16 gm.
Carbohydrate: 57 gm. – Cholesterol: 10 mg. – Fiber: high

Cheesy Bean Pie

 Your favorite beans and rice, baked in a pie, spiced up with chili powder and cumin, and topped with cheese.

15-ounce can kidney beans, black beans,
   or Great Northern beans, drained

1 1/2 cups cooked rice

1 egg, lightly beaten

1 cup fat-free milk

1 teaspoon Worcestershire sauce

1 teaspoon dry mustard

1 teaspoon chili powder

1/4 teaspoon cumin

1/2 teaspoon freshly ground pepper

1/2 teaspoon salt

2 cups grated low-fat cheddar cheese, divided

Preheat oven to 325°. Grease a 9-inch pie pan. Combine beans, rice, egg, milk, Worcestershire sauce, dry mustard, chili powder, cumin, pepper, salt, and 1 cup of the cheese in a large bowl. Pour into pie pan. Top with remaining cup of grated cheese. Bake for 40 to 50 minutes or until lightly browned.

Serves 4

Nutrition Information per serving:
Calories: 260 – Fat: 9 gm. – Protein: 16 gm.
Carbohydrate: 28 gm. – Cholesterol: 50 mg. – Fiber: very high

Fried Rice

 The next time you prepare rice, make extra for a quick fried rice dinner. The ginger and soy sauce are key ingredients. Make your own fried rice creation with other additions such as water chestnuts, shrimp, chicken, or pork.

2 tablespoons vegetable oil, divided

4 cups cold cooked rice

4 green onions

1 large carrot, peeled and finely chopped

1 stalk celery, finely chopped

1 teaspoon minced fresh gingerroot

1/2 pound fresh mushrooms, sliced

1/2 cup frozen green peas

2 tablespoons dry sherry

1/4 cup soy sauce

1 teaspoon sugar

2 eggs, lightly beaten

salt and pepper to taste

In a large nonstick skillet heat 1 tablespoon vegetable oil. Add rice and cook over medium-hot heat until rice is lightly browned and slightly crisp. Stir occasionally. While rice is browning heat 1 tablespoon oil in a medium nonstick skillet. Add onions, carrots, celery, gingerroot, and mushrooms. Cook over medium heat, stirring occasionally, until vegetables are tender. Add peas. In a small custard cup combine sherry, soy sauce, and sugar. Pour into skillet with vegetables and stir to mix. Combine vegetables with rice. Increase heat and pour eggs into hot rice mixture. Stir constantly and cook until eggs have set. Reduce heat to low. Adjust seasoning with extra soy sauce, salt, and pepper to taste.

Note: This recipe does not work well unless the rice has been cooked and chilled ahead of time. It is also important to use a nonstick skillet when browning the rice.

Serves 6

Nutrition Information per serving:
Calories: 290 – Fat: 6 gm. – Protein: 8 gm.
Carbohydrate: 51 gm. – Cholesterol: 30 mg. – Fiber: high

Lentil Stew

 Lentils come in many different colors. Pick your favorite and add rich flavor with Italian seasonings. The combination of vegetables, seasonings, and sherry make this a "keeper recipe" and it can be made in less than an hour.

2 cups lentils

6 cups (48 ounces) vegetable broth
    or low-fat chicken broth

1 tablespoon olive oil

2 large onions, chopped

3 large carrots, peeled and chopped

2 stalks celery, chopped

15-ounce can Italian-style diced tomatoes

1/2 teaspoon thyme

1/2 teaspoon marjoram

1/2 teaspoon oregano

1/2 cup minced fresh parsley

1/4 cup dry sherry

salt to taste

freshly ground pepper to taste

1/2 cup freshly grated Parmesan cheese,
    optional

Wash lentils in a colander under running water. In a large pan combine lentils with broth. Bring to a boil. Reduce heat, cover, and simmer for 30 minutes or until lentils are soft. Meanwhile heat olive oil in medium skillet. Cook onions, carrots, and celery over medium heat until onions are translucent. Add vegetable mixture to cooked lentils. Add tomatoes, thyme, marjoram, oregano, and parsley. Bring to a slow boil and cook until vegetables are tender and soup reaches desired consistency. Add extra broth for a thinner soup. Add sherry just before serving. Add salt and pepper to taste. Top each serving with grated Parmesan cheese if desired.

Serves 8

Nutrition Information per serving:
Calories: 325 – Fat: 5 gm. – Protein: 18 gm.
Carbohydrate: 52 gm. – Cholesterol: 5 mg. – Fiber: very high

Marinara Sauce

 Real homemade flavor, yet so easy. This is a great recipe to make ahead and it keeps for days in the refrigerator. Just reheat for a quick supper.

1 tablespoon olive oil	1 teaspoon basil
1 large onion, finely chopped	1/2 teaspoon oregano
3 cloves garlic, minced	1/4 teaspoon thyme
30 ounces tomato sauce	1/2 teaspoon freshly ground pepper
30-ounce can Italian-style stewed tomatoes	1 teaspoon sugar
1/2 cup water	salt to taste
2 bay leaves	

In a large heavy saucepan heat oil. Add onions and cook over medium heat until translucent. Add garlic and cook 1 minute. Add tomato sauce, canned tomatoes, water, bay leaves, basil, oregano, thyme, and pepper. Bring to a boil. Reduce heat and simmer slowly for about 1 hour or until sauce reaches desired thickness. Add sugar and salt to taste. Remove bay leaves. Serve over pasta.

Serves 4

Nutrition Information per serving without pasta:
Calories: 175 – Fat: 4 gm. – Protein: 6 gm.
Carbohydrate: 29 – Cholesterol: 0 mg. – Fiber: very high

Mashed Potato and Red Pepper Pizza

 This is sure to become a family favorite. The garlic potatoes topped with Italian-seasoned peppers and mushrooms make this a unique and memorable pizza.

10-ounce can refrigerated pizza crust

1 tablespoon olive oil

1 medium red bell pepper, thinly sliced

1/2 pound fresh mushrooms

1 medium tomato, seeded and chopped

1/4 teaspoon basil

1/2 teaspoon oregano

2/3 cup water

1/8 teaspoon salt

2/3 cup garlic-flavor mashed potato flakes

2 tablespoons milk

1/3 pound mozzarella cheese, shredded

crushed red pepper flakes, optional

Preheat oven to 425°. Lightly grease a cookie sheet or pizza pan. Unroll pizza dough and pat evenly onto the pan in about a 10-inch circle. Bake for 5 minutes. Remove from oven and set aside. While crust is baking heat oil in a medium skillet. Over medium heat cook peppers, mushrooms, tomatoes, basil, and oregano until vegetables are tender (about 5 minutes). Remove from heat. In a small saucepan, bring water to a boil. Add salt, mashed potato flakes, and milk. Stir with a fork. Spread potatoes over pizza crust. Spread pepper and mushroom mixture evenly over potatoes. Top with cheese. Bake for 10 minutes or until crust is light brown and cheese is melted. Top with crushed red pepper flakes if desired.

Note: Other favorite pizza toppings such as black olives and Canadian bacon can be added.

Serves 3

Nutrition Information per serving:
Calories: 400 – Fat: 15 gm. – Protein: 22 gm.
Carbohydrate: 44 gm. – Cholesterol: 40 mg. – Fiber: medium

Pasta Primavera

 You won't believe this wonderful creamy dish with a hint of nutmeg is so low in fat. It tastes and feels like a full fat dish.

8 ounces pasta shells or linguine	1 cup snow peas
1 tablespoon butter or margarine	1/2 cup low-fat chicken broth
1 medium onion, finely chopped	2 tablespoons flour
1/2 pound fresh mushrooms, sliced	1 1/2 cups fat-free half-and-half
2 cloves garlic, minced	1/4 teaspoon nutmeg
2 cups fresh broccoli florets	1/2 cup grated fresh Parmesan cheese, divided
1 cup fresh cauliflower florets	salt to taste
1 medium red pepper	freshly ground pepper to taste

Cook pasta in a large saucepan of boiling water just until tender. Drain and set aside. In a large skillet, heat butter over medium heat. Add onions and cook until translucent. Add mushrooms and garlic. Cook until mushrooms are tender. Add broccoli, cauliflower, red pepper, and snow peas. In a shaker combine chicken broth with flour. Add broth, half-and-half, and nutmeg to vegetables. Cook, stirring constantly, until mixture thickens. Reduce heat, cover pan, and cook 5 to 10 minutes or until vegetables are tender. Add cooked pasta and 1/4 cup of Parmesan cheese. Heat through. Adjust seasoning with salt and pepper. Top individual servings with remaining Parmesan cheese.

Serves 4

Nutrition Information per serving:
Calories: 435 – Fat: 7 gm. – Protein: 25 gm.
Carbohydrate: 68 gm. – Cholesterol: 20 mg. – Fiber: very high

Pasta with Artichokes and Black Olives

 So quick when you use canned spaghetti sauce, but make it special with your creative seasoning touches.

1/2 pound penne rigate (small tube-shaped pasta)

1/2 tablespoon olive oil

1 pound fresh mushrooms, sliced

2 cloves garlic, minced

9 ounces frozen artichokes

3/4 cup pitted black olives, halved

24 ounces canned spaghetti sauce of your choice

1/4 cup chopped fresh basil

1/4 cup grated Parmesan cheese

In a large saucepan of lightly salted boiling water add pasta. Cook until tender but do not overcook. Drain. Stir in 1 tablespoon of the warm cooking liquid and place on warm platter. (This keeps pasta from sticking together.) Meanwhile in a large nonstick skillet, heat olive oil. Over medium heat cook mushrooms until tender. Add garlic and cook 1 minute. Add artichokes, olives, spaghetti sauce, and basil. Bring to a boil, reduce heat, and simmer for 5 minutes. Spoon sauce over warm pasta. Top with grated cheese.

Serves 4

Nutrition Information per serving:
Calories: 520 – Fat: 14 gm. – Protein: 17 gm.
Carbohydrate: 81 gm. – Cholesterol: 10 mg. – Fiber: very high

Red Pepper Quesadillas

 A surprisingly tasty supper meal with southwestern seasonings, but great served as an appetizer too.

1 tablespoon vegetable oil

1 large onion, sliced

1 large red bell pepper, chopped

1/2 cup frozen corn

1 teaspoon ground cumin

1 tablespoon fresh cilantro, chopped

1 teaspoon coriander

1/4 teaspoon cayenne pepper

1 teaspoon medium-hot chili powder

15-ounce can black beans, drained

2 tablespoons chicken broth

8 medium flour tortillas

vegetable oil cooking spray

1/2 cup salsa

1 cup part-skim mozzarella cheese, grated

Garnishes: salsa, guacamole, fat-free sour cream

In a large skillet, heat oil. Add onions and red peppers. Cook until onions are translucent and peppers are tender. Add corn, cumin, cilantro, coriander, cayenne pepper, and chili powder. Cook for 5 minutes. In a small bowl, mash black beans and chicken broth together. Add to skillet and heat. Taste and adjust seasoning.

Spray one side of flour tortillas with cooking spray. Heat a small nonstick skillet over medium heat. Lay a tortilla, oil side down, in the skillet. Spoon a layer of bean mixture on tortilla. Top with 2 tablespoons of salsa and 1/4 cup grated cheese. Cover with another tortilla. Spray top of tortilla with cooking spray. Cook tortilla until brown on one side and flip to the other side. Remove from pan and cut into quarters. Repeat with remaining tortillas. Serve with extra salsa, guacamole, and sour cream.

Serves 4

Nutrition Information per serving:
Calories: 475 – Fat: 15 gm. – Protein: 21 gm.
Carbohydrate: 64 gm. – Cholesterol: 20 mg. – Fiber: very high

Ricotta and Spinach Stuffed Pasta Shells

 Easy to make with a jar of purchased marinara sauce or make your own homemade sauce.

18 jumbo pasta shells (8 ounces)

1 teaspoon olive oil

3 cloves garlic, minced

10 ounces frozen chopped spinach, squeezed dry

2 cups fat-free ricotta cheese

1/4 cup dry bread crumbs

1/2 teaspoon nutmeg

1/2 teaspoon white pepper

1 egg, lightly beaten

1 cup freshly grated Parmesan cheese, divided

4 cups prepared marinara sauce, divided*

1/4 cup chopped fresh parsley

Preheat oven to 350°. Grease a 9 x 13 inch baking pan or six small individual baking dishes. Cook pasta shells in a large pot of boiling salted water until al dente. Rinse with cold water and drain. Set aside. Combine oil and garlic in medium saucepan. Cook over low heat 1 minute. Remove from heat. Add spinach, ricotta cheese, bread crumbs, nutmeg, white pepper, egg, and 1/4 cup Parmesan cheese. Mix well. Stuff each shell with about 2 tablespoons of the cheese mixture. Spoon 1 cup of the marinara sauce in bottom of baking pan. Arrange shells in a single layer on top of the sauce. Sprinkle with 1/4 cup of cheese. Spoon remaining sauce on top of shells. Top with remaining 1/2 cup of cheese. Bake for 30 minutes or until shells are heated through. Garnish with parsley.

*If you prefer to make your own sauce, the recipe for Marinara Sauce is on page 131. This meal can be prepared ahead and baked at a later time. Cover pan and refrigerate until ready to serve. Add 10 minutes to the baking time or bake until heated through.

Serves 6

Nutrition Information per serving:
Calories: 410 – Fat: 12 gm. – Protein: 27 gm.
Carbohydrate: 53 gm. – Cholesterol: 55 mg. – Fiber: medium

Southwestern Bean Chili

 This chili is a great full-flavored meal with lots of beans and tomatoes, and seasoned with chili powder, hot chiles, and cumin. Even meat lovers will like it!

2 tablespoons cooking oil

2 medium onions, chopped

1/2 medium green pepper, chopped

1 medium red pepper, chopped

2 stalks celery, chopped

3 cloves garlic, minced

30-ounce can stewed tomatoes

15 ounces vegetable broth or low-fat
  chicken broth

1/2 teaspoon oregano flakes

1 teaspoon cumin

1 tablespoon chili powder

1/2 teaspoon freshly ground black pepper

16-ounce can kidney beans

16-ounce can white beans

16-ounce can black beans, drained and rinsed

1 fresh jalapeño chile, seeds removed, minced
  (optional)

1 cup frozen corn

salt to taste

Heat oil in a large saucepan over medium heat. Add onions and cook until translucent. Reduce heat to low and add peppers, celery, and garlic. Cook until tender. Add stewed tomatoes, broth, oregano, cumin, chili powder, black pepper, kidney beans, white beans, black beans, and jalapeño chile. Bring to a boil. Reduce heat and simmer for 30 to 40 minutes. Add corn and cook for an additional 5 minutes. Adjust seasoning with salt and extra pepper or extra chiles if desired.

Topping ideas: Serve with fresh cilantro, sour cream, or shredded cheese.

Note: The kidney beans and white beans do not need to be drained. It is best to drain and rinse the black beans because the dark color of the liquid does not enhance the appearance of the chili.

Serves 8

Nutrition Information per serving:
Calories: 280 – Fat: 5 gm. – Protein: 13 gm.
Carbohydrate: 46 – Cholesterol: 0 mg. – Fiber: very high

Spinach, Feta Cheese, and Noodle Squares

 This spinach and noodle dish creates a tasty meatless meal or a side dish. It can also be cut in small pieces and served as bite-sized appetizers.

1 tablespoon olive oil

1 large onion, finely chopped

4 cloves garlic, minced

10 ounces frozen spinach, thawed and squeezed dry

2 eggs, lightly beaten

8 ounces feta cheese, crumbled

1 cup low-fat cottage cheese

1/2 cup grated fresh Parmesan cheese, divided

1/2 teaspoon freshly ground pepper

1/4 teaspoon crushed red pepper

1/2 teaspoon oregano

1 pound fine egg noodles

butter-flavor cooking spray

Preheat oven to 375°. Butter a 9 x 13 inch nonstick baking pan. In a medium skillet, heat oil. Cook onions over medium heat until translucent. Add garlic and cook 1 minute. Remove from heat. In a medium bowl, combine onions and garlic with dry spinach, eggs, feta cheese, cottage cheese, 1/4 cup Parmesan cheese, pepper, crushed red pepper, and oregano. Stir until well mixed. Cook noodles in a large pot of salted water for 3 to 4 minutes or until al dente. (Do not overcook noodles.) Drain well. Spoon half of the noodles into the baking pan. Press down with back of the spoon. Spoon spinach mixture over the top and smooth out evenly. Arrange remaining noodles on top. Press down with back of the spoon. Spray lightly with butter-flavored cooking spray. Sprinkle with remaining Parmesan cheese. Bake for 30 minutes or until golden brown. Cool 10 to 20 minutes before cutting. Serves 8 for a meal or cut into small squares for appetizers.

Note: For an 8 x 8 inch pan, prepare one-half of the recipe.

Serves 8

Nutrition Information per serving:
Calories: 380 – Fat: 13 gm. – Protein: 20 gm.
Carbohydrate: 45 gm. – Cholesterol: 130 mg. – Fiber: medium

Spinach Mushroom Quiche

 This quiche seasoned with nutmeg and a touch of cayenne pepper would also be good made with broccoli in place of the spinach.

9-inch pie crust

1 tablespoon butter or margarine

1 medium onion, finely chopped

1/2 pound fresh mushrooms, sliced

1 tablespoon flour

1/4 teaspoon nutmeg

1/8 teaspoon cayenne pepper

1 teaspoon salt

1 teaspoon Worcestershire sauce

1 1/4 cups skim milk, divided

2 eggs, lightly beaten

10 ounces frozen spinach, thawed and squeezed dry

1 cup grated low-fat Swiss cheese

grated nutmeg for garnish

Preheat oven to 400°. Prick bottom of unbaked pie shell and bake for 5 minutes. Set aside. Reduce oven temperature to 375°. In a frying pan, melt butter. Cook onions and mushrooms over medium heat until onions are translucent and liquid from mushrooms has evaporated. In a shaker combine flour, nutmeg, pepper, salt, Worcestershire sauce, and 1/2 cup milk. Add to skillet and bring to a boil, stirring constantly. Remove from heat and add remaining 3/4 cup milk and eggs. Mix well. Stir in spinach and Swiss cheese. Pour into partially baked pie shell. Sprinkle with grated nutmeg. Bake for 45 to 60 minutes or until knife inserted in the center comes out clean.

Serves 6

Nutrition Information per serving:
Calories: 260 – Fat: 13 gm. – Protein: 13 gm.
Carbohydrate: 23 gm. – Cholesterol: 80 mg. – Fiber: low

Swiss Vegetable Quiche

 This is a gorgeous quiche with a surprise. It is made with a rice crust, eliminating the usual high-fat crust. The thyme and oregano seasonings complement the vegetables.

Crust:

2 cups cooked rice

1 egg, lightly beaten

1/4 teaspoon salt

1/4 teaspoon white pepper

1/4 cup shredded low-fat Swiss
    cheese

Filling:

16-ounce bag frozen broccoli, cauliflower,
    and red pepper mix

1 cup shredded low-fat Swiss cheese

3 eggs, lightly beaten

12 ounces evaporated skim milk

3/4 teaspoon thyme

1/2 teaspoon oregano

1/2 teaspoon salt

1/4 teaspoon cayenne pepper

1/4 teaspoon freshly ground black pepper

Preheat oven to 350°. Thoroughly grease a 9-inch pie pan. In a small bowl mix all crust ingredients. Spoon into pie pan and pat firmly onto the bottom and up the sides. Thaw vegetables in microwave. Spoon into rice crust. Top with 1 cup Swiss cheese. In a medium bowl combine eggs, milk, thyme, oregano, salt, cayenne pepper, and black pepper. Pour over vegetables in pie pan. Bake for 40 to 45 minutes or until set and lightly browned. Let stand 10 minutes before cutting. Serve with extra freshly ground pepper if desired.

Serves 6

Nutrition Information per serving:
Calories: 275 – Fat: 6 gm. – Protein: 19 gm.
Carbohydrate: 37 gm. – Cholesterol: 130 mg. – Fiber: high

Vegetable and Black Bean Fajitas

 Blackened peppers are combined with beans and Mexican spices.

1 tablespoon olive oil

2 small zucchini, sliced

2 medium onions, sliced

2 cloves garlic, minced

1 red pepper

1 green pepper

3 tomatoes, seeded and chopped

15-ounce can black beans, drained

1 tablespoon fresh cilantro, chopped

1 teaspoon chili powder

1/2 teaspoon cumin

4 12-inch flour tortillas

1 cup fat-free sour cream

1 cup tomato salsa

In a medium skillet heat olive oil. Cook zucchini and onion over medium heat until onions are translucent. Add garlic and cook 1 minute. Remove from heat and set aside. Blacken peppers under hot broiler or over gas flame. (See page 15 for specific directions.) Remove blackened skin of peppers. Slice the peppers and add to the zucchini and onions. Stir in chopped tomatoes, beans, cilantro, chili powder, and cumin. Heat over low heat until warm. To serve, spoon one-quarter of the mixture down the center of each warm tortilla. Fold in edges. Serve with sour cream and salsa.

Note: Blackened peppers can be purchased in jars.

Serves 4

Nutrition Information per serving:
Calories: 370 – Fat: 9 gm. – Protein: 13 gm.
Carbohydrate: 59 gm. – Cholesterol: 10 mg. – Fiber: high

Veggie Rice

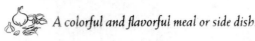 *A colorful and flavorful meal or side dish.*

1 cup long-grain white rice

1 teaspoon chicken bouillon

2 tablespoons olive oil

2 medium carrots, peeled and finely chopped

1 small onion, finely chopped

2 small zucchini, finely chopped

2 cloves garlic, minced

11-ounce can corn, drained

1 teaspoon dill weed

1 teaspoon dry mustard

1/4 teaspoon freshly ground pepper

salt to taste

1/4 teaspoon cayenne pepper, optional

In a medium saucepan combine rice, bouillon, and 2 cups water. Bring to a boil; cover and simmer for 20 minutes. While rice is cooking, heat oil in a medium skillet. Add carrots, cover pan, and cook over medium heat until tender. Add onions and zucchini and cook until onions are translucent. Add garlic and cook 1 minute. Add corn, dill weed, dry mustard, and pepper. Combine vegetables with cooked rice. Add salt and cayenne pepper to taste.

Serves 4

Nutrition Information per serving:
Calories: 315 – Fat: 8 gm. – Protein: 4 gm.
Carbohydrate: 57 – Cholesterol: 0 mg. – Fiber: high

Meats

Bavarian Pork Chops

 Full flavored with garlic and beer. Serve with buttered noodles or boiled red potatoes.

1 1/2 pounds lean pork loin chops

2 tablespoons flour

1/2 teaspoon salt

1/2 teaspoon thyme

1/4 teaspoon cayenne pepper

2 tablespoons cooking oil

1/2 cup chopped green onions

2 cloves garlic, minced

1 pound fresh mushrooms, sliced

12 ounces beer, room temperature

1/4 cup minced fresh parsley

Cut any visible fat from pork chops. Place chops in plastic bag. Add flour, salt, thyme, and pepper to bag and shake until well coated. In a large heavy skillet, heat oil. Brown chops quickly on both sides and remove from pan. Add onions and garlic to skillet and cook over medium heat for 2 minutes. Add mushrooms and cook until mushrooms are tender. Return meat to pan and add beer. Bring to a boil. Reduce heat, cover pan, and simmer for 15 to 20 minutes. Garnish with fresh parsley when ready to serve.

Note: For a thicker sauce, mix 1 tablespoon flour with 1/4 cup of water in a shaker. Stir into sauce and bring to a boil, stirring constantly.

Serves 4

Nutrition Information per serving:
Calories: 335 – Fat: 18 gm. – Protein: 30 gm.
Carbohydrate: 13 gm. – Cholesterol: 85 mg. – Fiber: low

Beef and Bean Stuffed Peppers

 Pick some peppers of each color for a beautiful presentation.
Add extra green chiles if you like it hot.

4 large red, yellow, or green bell peppers

3/4 pound extra lean ground beef

1 medium onion, chopped

15-ounce can kidney beans

15-ounce can tomato puree

1/4 cup green chiles, finely chopped

2 teaspoons chili powder

1/2 teaspoon cumin

1/4 cup minced fresh parsley

Preheat oven to 350°. Grease a 9 x 13 inch baking pan. Cut peppers in half lengthwise. Remove seeds and membranes. Place peppers cut sides up in the baking pan. Brown ground beef in heavy saucepan. Add onions and cook until translucent. Drain any excess fat. Stir in all remaining ingredients except parsley. Bring to a boil. Reduce heat and simmer 10 minutes, stirring frequently. Add water if mixture is too thick. Spoon mixture into peppers. Cover and bake for 40 to 45 minutes or until peppers are tender. Arrange on platter. Garnish with parsley.

Serves 4

Nutrition Information per serving:
Calories: 365 – Fat: 15 gm. – Protein: 24 gm.
Carbohydrate: 34 gm. – Cholesterol: 65 mg. – Fiber: very high

Beef and Veggie Burger

 These taste even better than plain hamburgers.
Kids love them and they will be getting their vegetables, too!

1/2 tablespoon butter or margarine

1 small onion, finely chopped

1 cup finely shredded or grated carrots

2 tablespoons beef or chicken broth

1 egg, lightly beaten

1 pound extra lean ground beef

1 teaspoon salt

1/4 teaspoon pepper

1/4 teaspoon thyme

cooking oil spray

In a medium skillet, melt butter. Add onions and cook until translucent. Add carrots and broth. Cover and cook until carrots are tender. Remove from heat. In a large bowl, combine onions, carrots, egg, ground beef, salt, pepper, and thyme. Mix well. Shape into 6 patties. Spray skillet with cooking oil spray. Cook patties over medium heat, partially covered, until brown on both sides and completely cooked on the inside.

Note: If you like garlic, cook minced garlic with the onions and carrots.

Serves 6

Nutrition Information per serving:
Calories: 200 – Fat: 14 gm. – Protein: 15 gm.
Carbohydrate: 3 gm. – Cholesterol: 80 mg. – Fiber: low

Beef Burgundy

 This is one of those times when canned soup in a recipe makes dinner so easy and yet so good. Your family will love it and there will be enough left over for another meal. It is also a crowd pleaser for large groups of guests.

1 tablespoon corn oil

2 large onions, sliced

3 pounds lean beef, cubed

1 teaspoon pepper, coarsely ground

2 cloves garlic, minced

1 pound fresh mushrooms, halved

1 cup Burgundy or dry red wine

10 ounces cream of mushroom soup, undiluted

1 ounce onion soup mix (1 envelope)

10 ounces canned beef consommé

24 ounces egg noodles, uncooked

1/4 cup minced fresh parsley

Preheat oven to 325°. Choose a large, heavy pan that can be used on the stove and in the oven. Heat oil in the pan. Cook onions over medium heat until onions are translucent. Add beef and cook until brown, stirring occasionally. Add pepper, garlic, and mushrooms. Cook about 3 minutes, stirring occasionally, until mushrooms have softened. Add wine, mushroom soup, dry onion soup, and beef consommé. Cover pan. Bake for 1 1/2 hours or until meat is tender and sauce has thickened. Check occasionally and add water if sauce gets too thick. Twenty minutes before serving, cook egg noodles in boiling water until tender. Drain. Serve beef and sauce over noodles. Garnish with minced parsley.

Serves 10

Nutrition Information per serving:
Calories: 490 – Fat: 12 gm. – Protein: 41 gm.
Carbohydrate: 55 gm. – Cholesterol: 140 mg. – Fiber: medium

Beef Tenderloin with Red Wine Mushroom Sauce

 The interesting combination of cloves and allspice in a mushroom wine sauce raises a plain steak to new heights.

2 pounds beef tenderloin or other lean steak	1 teaspoon freshly ground pepper
14 ounces beef broth	1/2 teaspoon ground cloves
1 1/2 tablespoons cornstarch	1/2 teaspoon ground allspice
1/4 cup dry red wine	2 teaspoons brown sugar
1 teaspoon marjoram	8-ounce can sliced mushrooms, drained

Trim fat and white membrane from beef tenderloin. In a small saucepan, combine beef broth and cornstarch. Bring to a boil and stir until sauce thickens. Reduce heat and add wine, marjoram, pepper, cloves, allspice, and brown sugar. Cook over medium heat for 5 minutes. Cool to room temperature. Place cooled marinade and beef in a zipping plastic bag. Seal and refrigerate for several hours.

When ready to serve, preheat grill to high heat. Remove tenderloin from marinade and place on hot grill. Grill tenderloin until brown on the outside and the meat reaches the desired temperature in the middle. While meat is on the grill pour reserved marinade into small saucepan. Add mushrooms and bring to a boil. Reduce heat and boil gently until meat is ready to serve. Serve meat on warm plates topped with mushroom sauce.

Serves 6

Nutrition Information per serving:
Calories: 315 – Fat: 12 gm. – Protein: 46 gm.
Carbohydrate: 5 gm. – Cholesterol: 100 mg. – Fiber: 0

Curried Beef Kabobs

 This is a unique, interesting seasoning mix for beef.
Serve with saffron rice for an elegant meal.

1 pound beef tenderloin

2 tablespoons corn oil

1/4 cup dry sherry

1/4 cup lemon juice

2 cloves garlic, minced

1 small onion, chopped

1 tablespoon fresh ginger, minced

1 teaspoon hot curry powder

1/2 tablespoon turmeric

1/2 teaspoon salt

1 large green pepper, cubed

1 large red pepper, cubed

8 small red potatoes, parboiled

8 large mushroom caps

4 medium cherry tomatoes

Cut meat into 2-inch cubes. In a small jar, combine corn oil, sherry, lemon juice, garlic, onion, ginger, curry powder, turmeric, and salt. Shake until mixed will. Pour into zipping bag and add cubed meat. Mix well. Seal bag and refrigerate 4 to 12 hours.

Preheat grill when ready to serve. Remove meat from marinade. Discard marinade. Use 4 large skewers. Alternate meat, peppers, potatoes, and mushrooms on skewers. End with a cherry tomato. Grill over hot coals, turning when necessary to prevent burning. Cook until meat is brown and cooked to desired temperature. Serve with Saffron Rice (see recipe on page 98).

Serves 4

Nutrition Information per serving:
Calories: 425 – Fat: 14 gm. – Protein: 28 gm.
Carbohydrate: 47 gm. – Cholesterol: 80 mg. – Fiber: medium

German Kraut and Pork Skillet Dinner

 Warm, savory cooking aromas signal a warm, hearty meal.

1 tablespoon cooking oil	1 tablespoon brown sugar
1 1/2 pounds extra lean boneless pork loin chops	1/2 teaspoon marjoram
	1/4 teaspoon rosemary
1/4 teaspoon salt	1/2 teaspoon caraway seed, optional
1/4 teaspoon pepper	1/4 teaspoon pepper
1 large onion, chopped	1 cup beer
27-ounce can sauerkraut	2 medium apples, cored and quartered

In a large skillet, heat oil. Sprinkle pork chops with salt and pepper. Brown pork chops over medium-hot heat. Reduce heat to medium and add onions. Cook onions until translucent. In a medium bowl combine sauerkraut, brown sugar, marjoram, rosemary, caraway seed, pepper, and beer. Mix well. Pour over pork chops. Cover pan and simmer for 45 minutes. Add apple wedges and simmer 10 minutes longer.

Serves 4

Nutrition Information per serving:
Calories: 400 – Fat: 12 gm. – Protein: 50 gm.
Carbohydrate: 24 gm. – Cholesterol: 150 mg. – Fiber: high

Ginger Pork and Broccoli Stir-Fry

 So easy, fast, and full of ginger. Other vegetables can be added to suit your taste or use up your leftovers.

1 pound pork tenderloin

3 tablespoons soy sauce

3 tablespoons apricot brandy or dry sherry

1 tablespoon cornstarch

1/2 teaspoon red pepper flakes

1/8 teaspoon ground ginger

2 tablespoons peanut oil

2 teaspoons minced fresh ginger

1 cup low-fat chicken stock

2 cups fresh broccoli florets

1/4 cup dry-roasted peanuts

Remove white membrane from pork tenderloin and cut meat into 1-inch strips. Set aside. (Note: Other cuts of lean pork can also be used.) In a small bowl, combine soy sauce, apricot brandy, cornstarch, red pepper flakes, and ground ginger. Pour mixture into a zipping plastic bag. Add pork. Marinate meat in refrigerator 1 to 4 hours. In a heavy nonstick skillet or wok, heat oil. Remove meat from bag and drain, saving marinade. Add meat and minced fresh ginger to the hot oil and cook until meat is brown. Reduce heat and add chicken stock, the reserved marinade, and broccoli. Cook, stirring constantly, until mixture thickens and broccoli is tender-crisp. Add more chicken stock if sauce is too thick. Top with peanuts and serve over cooked rice.

Serves 4

Nutrition Information per serving without the rice:
Calories: 300 – Fat: 15 gm. – Protein: 31 gm.
Carbohydrate: 10 gm. – Cholesterol: 75 mg. – Fiber: low

Ground Sirloin with Tarragon Mushroom Sauce

 Very lean ground meat can be dry but this tarragon sauce adds flavor and the needed moistness. The sauce is similar to a bearnaise sauce, but with much less butter. It can be served with other meats or with vegetarian dishes.

1 pound extra lean ground beef sirloin

1/2 teaspoon salt

1 tablespoon butter or margarine

1/4 cup minced shallots or onions

1 pound fresh mushrooms, sliced

1/2 teaspoon dried tarragon

1/4 teaspoon freshly ground pepper

2 tablespoons flour

1 1/2 cups low-fat beef broth, divided

2 tablespoons red wine

salt and pepper to taste

Form meat into 4 patties. Heat a nonstick skillet over low-medium heat. Sprinkle salt in the bottom of the skillet. Fry meat patties until brown and both sides are completely done in the middle. (No pink meat!) Meanwhile melt butter in medium saucepan. Add shallots and cook over medium heat for 2 minutes. Add mushrooms, tarragon, and pepper. Cook, stirring occasionally, until tender. In a shaker combine flour and 1/2 cup of the beef broth. Shake until well mixed. Pour into pan with mushrooms and add remaining beef broth. Bring to a boil, stirring constantly. Boil gently until thick and the desired consistency. Add red wine. Adjust seasoning with salt and pepper. Serve sauce over the cooked meat patties.

Serves 4

Nutrition Information per serving:
Calories: 315 – Fat: 17 gm. – Protein: 29 gm.
Carbohydrate: 10 gm. – Cholesterol: 90 mg. – Fiber: low

Honey Apricot Glazed Ham

 The apricot-flavored basting sauce with nutmeg and cloves is a perfect complement to ham.

1 cup honey	1/3 cup apricot jam
6-ounce can frozen concentrated orange juice, thawed	1/2 teaspoon nutmeg
	1/2 teaspoon cloves
1/3 cup soy sauce	3 pounds lean boneless ham

Preheat oven to 325°. In a small bowl, mix together honey, orange juice, soy sauce, jam, nutmeg, and cloves. Place ham in baking pan. Brush with sauce. Bake for 1 hour and baste several times during baking period.

Serve with Peach and Apple Salsa (see page 209).

Note: This sauce is also good on a grilled or fried ham steak.

Serves 8

Nutrition Information per serving:
Calories: 400 – Fat: 8 gm. – Protein: 34 gm.
Carbohydrate: 48 gm. – Cholesterol: 80 mg. – Fiber: low

Honey Mustard Glazed Pork Loin with Apples

A way to make an ordinary pork roast very special with very little extra effort.

3 pounds lean pork loin, rolled

2 tablespoons cooking oil

1 teaspoon allspice

1 teaspoon salt

1 teaspoon freshly ground black pepper

2 medium apples, peeled, cored, and finely diced

1/4 cup honey mustard

Preheat oven to 325°. Unroll roast and lay flat. Remove any visible fat. In a small bowl, combine oil, allspice, salt, and pepper. Spread half of spice mixture on the meat. Top with diced apples. Roll up roast tightly and tie securely. Place in baking pan. Spread remaining oil mixture on outside of the roast. Insert meat thermometer. Roast for 1 to 2 hours or until meat thermometer registers 170°. About 10 minutes before removing meat from oven, spread honey mustard over roast. Remove from oven and let roast rest 15 minutes before cutting. Serve additional mustard with meat.

Serves 6

Nutrition Information per serving:
Calories: 340 – Fat: 13 gm. – Protein: 48 gm.
Carbohydrate: 8 gm. – Cholesterol: 150 mg. – Fiber: low

Paella (Spanish Stew)

*Nontraditional without the clams, but add them if you like them.
You can also adapt this recipe to meet your taste with other vegetables,
meat, and seafood. Don't forget the saffron!*

1/2 pound chorizo or sausage of your choice

2 whole skinless, boneless chicken breasts

2 tablespoons olive oil

1 large onion, diced

2 cloves garlic, minced

1 medium red bell pepper, sliced

4 cups chicken stock

2 cups rice

1/2 teaspoon cayenne pepper or red pepper flakes

1 medium pinch saffron threads (about 35 threads)

salt to taste

1 cup canned garbanzo beans, drained (optional)

1 cup frozen green peas

1/2 pound cooked shrimp

Cut sausage and chicken breasts into bite-sized pieces. In a large, heavy skillet that has a cover, cook sausage pieces until brown and well done. Remove meat from pan and set aside. Discard fat. In the same pan, heat olive oil. Add chicken and cook over medium heat until brown. Remove chicken from pan. Set aside. Add onion, garlic, and red pepper to the pan. Cook over low heat until onions are translucent. (Do not allow garlic to brown.) Add chicken stock, rice, pepper, and saffron. Bring to a boil. Reduce heat, cover the pan, and simmer until rice is done and liquid has been absorbed. Add salt to taste. Add meat back to the pan. Add garbanzo beans (optional) and peas and stir gently. Top with cooked shrimp. Add extra chicken broth if it is too dry. Cover and cook over low heat until heated thoroughly.

Serves 8

Nutrition Information per serving:
Calories: 455 – Fat: 16 gm. – Protein: 30 gm.
Carbohydrate: 48 gm. – Cholesterol: 100 mg. – Fiber: medium

Paprika Pork Stew

 An old-fashioned meal that is perfect with mashed potatoes.

1 pound lean pork loin, cut in 2-inch cubes

1/4 cup flour

2 tablespoons paprika

1 teaspoon salt

1/2 teaspoon pepper

2 tablespoons cooking oil

1 large onion, sliced

2 cups low-fat chicken broth

1 large bay leaf

2 large carrots, peeled and sliced

1 medium rutabaga, optional

8 small red potatoes

1/2 cup fat-free sour cream

Remove any visible fat from pork loin and place meat cubes in plastic bag. Add flour, paprika, salt, and pepper to the bag. Shake well to coat meat. In a large, heavy pan, heat oil. Add meat and brown well over medium heat. Add onions and cook until translucent. Add chicken broth, bay leaf, carrots, rutabaga, and red potatoes. Bring to a boil. Reduce heat, cover pan, and simmer for about 1 to 1 1/2 hours or until meat and vegetables are tender. Check occasionally and add water if it gets too dry. If mixture needs to be thickened, mix 2 tablespoons of the flour mixture in 1/2 cup water to make a paste. Add to pan, stirring constantly. Bring to a boil and cook until desired consistency. When ready to serve, remove from heat and stir in sour cream.

Serves 6

Nutrition Information per serving:
Calories: 325 – Fat: 12 gm. – Protein: 20 gm.
Carbohydrate: 34 gm. – Cholesterol: 40 mg. – Fiber: high

Pineapple & Pepper Pork Kabobs

 Ginger, pineapple, and pork complement each other.

1 pound pork tenderloin, cut in 1 1/2-inch
    cubes

1 cup pineapple juice

1/3 cup dry sherry

2 tablespoons soy sauce

2 tablespoons brown sugar

1/2 teaspoon ground ginger

2 cloves garlic, minced

2 tablespoons cooking oil

1 cup pineapple chunks (canned or fresh)

1 medium green pepper, cut into cubes

1 medium red pepper, cut into cubes

1 medium yellow pepper, cut into cubes

1 tablespoon cornstarch

Place tenderloin cubes in large resealable plastic bag. In a small bowl combine pineapple juice, sherry, soy sauce, brown sugar, ginger, garlic, and oil. Mix and pour into bag with the pork. Seal bag and refrigerate for several hours or overnight. Turn occasionally.

When ready to serve, preheat grill to medium-hot heat. Remove pork from bag and thread alternately on skewers with pineapple and peppers. Grill until meat is brown on the outside and slightly pink on the inside. While meat is grilling, heat marinade in saucepan until mixture comes to a boil. In a custard cup combine cornstarch with 1 tablespoon water. Add to sauce and stir constantly until mixture boils and thickens. Reduce heat and keep warm. Serve warm sauce with the kabobs.

Serves 4

Nutrition Information per serving:
Calories: 335 – Fat: 11 gm. – Protein: 25 gm.
Carbohydrate: 29 gm. – Cholesterol: 70 mg. – Fiber: low

Pork Chops with Peach Cranberry Sauce

 You will get rave reviews for this warmly seasoned combination of peaches and cranberries, served with browned pork chops!

4 lean boneless loin pork chops (1 1/2 pounds)	1 tablespoon orange zest
1/2 teaspoon salt	1/4 teaspoon cinnamon
1/4 teaspoon pepper	1/4 teaspoon ground ginger
1 tablespoon cooking oil	1/8 teaspoon nutmeg
16-ounce can sliced peaches in light syrup	1/8 teaspoon allspice
1 cup fresh or frozen cranberries	1/4 teaspoon salt
3 tablespoons brown sugar	1 1/2 tablespoons cornstarch

Sprinkle chops with salt and pepper. Heat oil in large nonstick skillet over medium-high heat. Brown chops on both sides. In a small bowl combine peach syrup (set peaches aside), cranberries, brown sugar, orange zest, cinnamon, ginger, nutmeg, allspice, and salt. Stir to blend. Pour into pan and bring to a boil. Reduce heat, cover pan, and simmer for 10 to 15 minutes or until cranberries have popped and are tender. Remove pork chops from pan. Mix cornstarch in 1/4 cup cold water and add to the pan. Bring to a boil, stirring constantly, until mixture thickens. Add peaches to pan and heat through. Add water to thin if sauce is too thick. Serve warm sauce over chops.

Note: Raspberry-flavored canned peaches are especially good in this recipe.

Serves 4

Nutrition Information per serving:
Calories: 370 – Fat: 10 gm. – Protein: 36 gm.
Carbohydrate: 34 gm. – Cholesterol: 110 mg. – Fiber: medium

Rosemary Marinated Pork Kabobs

 Rosemary, marjoram, and thyme are the key flavors for the pork and vegetable marinade.

1 1/2 pounds pork top loin, cut in 2-inch cubes

1/4 cup olive oil

1/4 cup lemon juice

1 small onion, chopped

1 clove garlic, minced

1/2 teaspoon rosemary, crushed

1/2 teaspoon marjoram

1/2 teaspoon thyme

8 small red potatoes, cooked

8 large fresh mushrooms

2 small zucchini, cut in 2-inch cubes

12 medium cherry tomatoes

Place pork cubes in large resealable plastic bag. Add olive oil, lemon juice, onion, garlic, rosemary, marjoram, and thyme. Mix well, and refrigerate several hours or overnight.

When ready to serve, heat grill. Remove meat from marinade and reserve marinade. On skewers, alternate meat with vegetables. Place over hot grill. In a small saucepan, bring reserved marinade to a boil. Baste meat occasionally with heated marinade. Turn when needed to brown meat. Cook until meat is thoroughly cooked.

Serves 4

Nutrition Information per serving:
Calories: 510 – Fat: 10 gm. – Protein: 45 gm.
Carbohydrate: 60 gm. – Cholesterol: 90 mg. – Fiber: high

Rouladen (German Braised Beef Rolls)

 An old traditional German meal that looks difficult but is really easy to make.

1 1/2 pounds top round steak	2 tablespoons cooking oil
1/2 teaspoon salt	2 stalks celery, diced
1/2 teaspoon freshly ground pepper	2 large carrots, peeled and diced
6 tablespoons spicy prepared mustard	1 cup low-fat beef broth
6 large dill pickle halves	1 cup dry red wine
6 slices bacon, fried and crumbled	2 tablespoons flour
1/2 cup flour	parsley sprigs for garnish

Cut steak into 6 individual pieces about 4 ounces each, and pound to about 1/4-inch thick. Sprinkle with salt and pepper. Spread 1 tablespoon of mustard on each piece. Top each piece with a pickle and distribute bacon on top. Roll up each piece from narrow end, and tie firmly in 2 places with kitchen string or secure with toothpicks. Roll meat in flour. In a large heavy skillet, heat cooking oil. Brown meat over medium-hot heat. Add celery and carrots and cook 2 to 3 minutes. Add beef broth and wine. Simmer over low heat for 1 1/2 to 2 hours or until meat is tender. Check occasionally and add additional beef broth if needed.

Remove rolls to serving platter and keep warm. To prepare the gravy, strain liquid through a sieve or put mixture in a blender and mix until smooth. Return to pan. Combine 2 tablespoons flour with 1 cup water in a shaker. Pour slowly into pan, a little bit at a time, and stir continually until mixture boils. Add enough flour and water mixture to make gravy the desired thickness. Serve gravy with the meat rolls. Garnish with fresh parsley.

Serves 6

Nutrition Information per serving:
Calories: 360 – Fat: 19 gm. – Protein: 30 gm.
Carbohydrate: 11 gm. – Cholesterol: 75 mg. – Fiber: low

Saffron Strata

A classic dish to make ahead of time. For a meatless meal, substitute chopped broccoli for the ham.

1 medium pinch saffron threads (about 35 threads)

1 tablespoon warm water

5 slices lightly toasted bread, top crust removed, cubed

1/2 pound lean ham, cubed

1 cup low-fat grated cheddar cheese

3 eggs

1 1/2 cups fat-free milk

1/4 teaspoon white pepper

1/2 teaspoon salt

1/4 teaspoon grated nutmeg

Grease an 8 x 8 inch nonstick baking pan. In a cup, soak the saffron threads in warm water. Set aside. Place cubed bread in baking pan. Top with ham and grated cheese. In a large bowl, beat together eggs, milk, pepper, and salt. Add saffron. Pour over the bread, ham, and cheese. Top with grated nutmeg. Cover and refrigerate until ready to use.

Preheat oven to 350°. Bake for 1 hour or until wooden pick inserted in the middle comes out clean. Let set 10 minutes before cutting.

Note: Double the recipe for a 9 x 13 inch pan. Cooked sausage or bacon may be substituted for the ham.

Serves 4

Nutrition Information per serving:
Calories: 280 – Fat: 9 gm. – Protein: 28 gm.
Carbohydrate: 22 gm. – Cholesterol: 170 mg. – Fiber: very low

Spaghetti with Meat Sauce—A Family Favorite

 Super simple, but the combination of Italian spices makes this as good as more complex recipes.

1 pound extra lean ground beef	1/4 teaspoon thyme
1 large onion, finely chopped	1/4 teaspoon marjoram
1/2 teaspoon salt	1/4 teaspoon basil
1/2 teaspoon pepper	1/4 teaspoon rosemary, crushed
30 ounces tomato sauce	1/2 teaspoon sugar
1 cup water	1 pound spaghetti, cooked and drained
1 teaspoon oregano	

Brown meat and onions in a large heavy saucepan. Drain well. Sprinkle with salt and pepper. Add tomato sauce, water, and seasonings. Bring to a boil. Reduce heat and simmer uncovered for about 1 hour or until it reaches desired thickness. Stir occasionally. Add extra water if necessary. Add sugar and adjust seasonings with extra salt and pepper to taste. Serve with cooked spaghetti.

Note: An Italian seasoning blend can be substituted for the oregano, thyme, marjoram, basil, and rosemary.

Serves 6

Nutrition Information per serving:
Calories: 500 – Fat: 14 gm. – Protein: 26 gm.
Carbohydrate: 68 gm. – Cholesterol: 50 mg. – Fiber: high

Swedish Meatballs

 Swedish meatballs have a unique taste you can't quite define.
The secret is the combination of allspice, nutmeg, and cardamom.

Meatballs:

1 tablespoon vegetable oil

1 medium onion, finely chopped

1/2 cup low-fat chicken broth

1 cup dry bread crumbs

1 teaspoon salt

2 teaspoons sugar

1/2 teaspoon allspice

1/4 teaspoon nutmeg

1/4 teaspoon cardamom

1 pound lean ground beef

1 pound lean ground turkey white meat

Sauce:

1 tablespoon butter or margarine

1 tablespoon flour

1 teaspoon sugar

1 teaspoon salt

1/2 teaspoon white pepper

1/4 teaspoon nutmeg

1 cup evaporated fat-free milk

1 cup fat-free milk

1/2 cup fat-free sour cream

Preheat oven to 350°. In a small frying pan, heat oil. Cook onion over medium heat until translucent. In a large bowl combine onions with all remaining meatball ingredients. Add extra chicken broth if necessary to form balls that hold together. Form into small 3/4-inch balls. Place balls in a large baking pan. Bake for 20 to 25 minutes or until cooked throughout. (Ground meat must be cooked until brown without any pink in the middle.) Drain off fat. Place meatballs in chafing dish. To prepare the sauce, melt butter in a heavy saucepan. Stir in flour, sugar, salt, pepper, and nutmeg. Add evaporated milk and fat-free milk. Bring to a boil, and stir constantly with a wire whip until mixture thickens. Reduce heat and stir in sour cream. Heat through but do not boil. Add extra milk to thin if sauce gets too thick. Pour over warm meatballs. Serve warm.

Makes 48 small balls. Serves 8

Nutrition Information per serving:
Calories: 280 – Fat: 14 gm. – Protein: 24 gm.
Carbohydrate: 14 gm. – Cholesterol: 75 mg. – Fiber: low

Tarragon Pork Chops with Ginger Peach Sauce

 A wonderful brown sugar peach sauce served on tarragon-marinated pork.

1 1/2 pounds lean pork loin chops

1/2 cup white wine

1 tablespoon balsamic vinegar

1/4 teaspoon cayenne pepper

1 teaspoon tarragon

1/2 teaspoon salt

2 tablespoons vegetable oil, divided

15-ounce can sliced peaches in light syrup

1 tablespoon cornstarch

1 tablespoon brown sugar

1/2 teaspoon ginger

fresh tarragon for garnish, optional

Trim any visible fat from pork chops. Place in a large resealable plastic bag. In a small custard cup combine wine, vinegar, cayenne pepper, tarragon, salt, and 1 tablespoon oil. Pour mixture into bag with pork. Seal bag and refrigerate at least 2 hours or overnight.

In a large heavy nonstick skillet, heat 1 tablespoon oil over medium-hot heat. Drain marinade from pork and set marinade aside. Place pork in hot oil. Cook until lightly browned on one side; turn and cook on the other side until brown. Remove pork from pan and set aside. Drain peach syrup into a small custard cup. Stir cornstarch, brown sugar, and ginger into peach syrup. Pour peach syrup and reserved marinade back into the pan. Cook until mixture comes to a boil and thickens. Add peaches and pork chops to pan. Simmer 10 minutes or until pork is thoroughly cooked. Serve peach sauce over pork chops. Garnish with fresh tarragon.

Serves 4

Nutrition Information per serving:
Calories: 365 – Fat: 13 gm. – Protein: 36 gm.
Carbohydrate: 26 gm. – Cholesterol: 110 mg. – Fiber: low

Teriyaki Pork Tenderloin

 This is my family's absolute favorite meal and every time I serve it for company, they request the recipe.

3 pounds pork tenderloin	1 medium onion, sliced
1 cup corn oil	2 cloves garlic, minced
1/2 cup soy sauce	2 teaspoons ground ginger
1/2 cup dry sherry	

Remove fat and white membrane from pork tenderloin. Place pork tenderloins in resealable plastic bag. In a large jar combine oil, soy sauce, sherry, onion, garlic, and ginger. Cover and shake until mixed. Pour into bag with meat. Seal bag and refrigerate several hours or overnight.

When ready to serve, heat charcoal grill to hot heat. Remove meat from marinade and discard marinade. Grill tenderloin about 20 minutes or until brown on all sides and slightly pink in the inside (160° on the meat thermometer). Remove from heat and let meat rest at room temperature for 15 minutes before slicing.

Serves 6

Nutrition Information per serving:
Calories: 300 – Fat: 10 gm. – Protein: 50 gm.
Carbohydrate: 3 gm. – Cholesterol: 150 mg. – Fiber: very low

Poultry and Fish

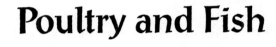

Baked Haddock with Tartar Sauce

 An easy, healthy fish dinner with homemade low-fat tartar sauce.

1/4 cup butter or margarine

2 tablespoons minced fresh parsley

1/2 teaspoon dill weed or tarragon

1/4 teaspoon nutmeg

2 pounds haddock fillets

1/2 teaspoon salt

1/2 teaspoon freshly ground black pepper

1/2 cup dry bread crumbs

1/4 teaspoon paprika

Preheat oven to 350°. Butter an 11 x 9 inch baking pan. In a small saucepan, melt butter and add parsley, dill weed, and nutmeg. Set aside. Season haddock with salt and pepper and place in baking pan. Brush butter mixture on both sides of the fish. Sprinkle bread crumbs over fish. Sprinkle with paprika. Bake for 15 to 20 minutes or until fish flakes easily with a fork and is cooked thoroughly. Serve with homemade tartar sauce (see page 214).

Note: Croutons can be ground in a food processor to make flavorful bread crumbs.

Serves 4

Nutrition Information per serving:
Calories: 320 – Fat: 13 gm. – Protein: 44 gm.
Carbohydrate: 6 gm. – Cholesterol: 160 mg. – Fiber: very low

Basil Mustard Grilled Chicken

 Serve as a hot entrée or chill the chicken and serve on a Caesar salad.

4 boned and skinned chicken breasts

1/4 cup olive oil

1/4 cup balsamic vinegar

2 tablespoons Dijon mustard

2 teaspoons basil

1 clove garlic, minced

1/4 teaspoon cayenne pepper

Place chicken breasts in resealable plastic bag. Add all remaining ingredients to the bag. Seal bag and mix well. Refrigerate several hours or overnight.

When ready to serve, heat grill to medium heat. Remove chicken from marinade and grill until brown and thoroughly done. Baste occasionally with marinade. Discard remaining marinade.

Serves 4

Nutrition Information per serving:
Calories: 220 – Fat: 6 gm. – Protein: 39 gm.
Carbohydrate: 2 gm. – Cholesterol: 100 mg. – Fiber: 0

Black Beans with Cilantro Chicken

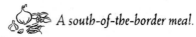 *A south-of-the-border meal.*

1 tablespoon cooking oil

4 skinless chicken breasts, diced

1/4 teaspoon salt

1/4 teaspoon cayenne pepper

6 green onions, chopped

1 cup diced celery

1/2 cup diced red bell pepper

2 cloves garlic, minced

15-ounce can black beans, drained

1 cup frozen corn

2 tablespoons chopped cilantro

1/2 cup salsa

1/4 cup chicken broth

In a large skillet heat oil. Place chicken in pan and sprinkle with salt and pepper. Brown on both sides over medium heat. Remove chicken from pan. Keep warm and set aside. Add onions, celery, and peppers to the pan. Cook over medium heat until onions are tender. Add garlic and cook 1 minute. Add beans, corn, cilantro, and salsa. Stir to mix. Place chicken back in pan. Cover and simmer over low heat 20 to 30 minutes or until chicken is completely done. Add chicken broth if mixture is too thick.

Serves 4

Nutrition Information per serving:
Calories: 310 – Fat: 7 gm. – Protein: 33 gm.
Carbohydrate: 29 gm. – Cholesterol: 65 mg. – Fiber: high

Bourbon Basted Salmon

 This may be the best salmon you have ever tasted. It browns beautifully and has a slightly sweet flavor. It is fantastic served either hot or cold.

3/4–1 pound salmon fillets or steaks

Marinade:

1/4 cup brown sugar

2 tablespoons vegetable oil

3 tablespoons bourbon

3 tablespoons chopped onion

2 tablespoons soy sauce

1/2 teaspoon ground ginger or

    1 tablespoon minced gingerroot

In a small bowl, combine marinade ingredients. Pour marinade into a resealable bag. Add salmon. Refrigerate 1 to 6 hours.

Remove salmon from marinade. In a nonstick frying pan with a small amount of cooking oil, fry salmon over low to medium heat. Fry until salmon is brown on both sides and thoroughly done. (The salmon browns quickly because there is sugar in the marinade.)

Note: The salmon may also be grilled over charcoal but watch carefully. It will burn easily.

Serves 2

Nutrition Information per serving:
Calories: 325 – Fat: 12 gm. – Protein: 35 gm.
Carbohydrate: 19 gm. – Cholesterol: 120 mg. – Fiber: 0

Chicken Cacciatore

 Another great way to enjoy those healthy tomatoes. The unusual combination of allspice, thyme, and peppers makes this a memorable meal.

2 tablespoons olive oil

4 boneless, skinless chicken breast halves

1/4 teaspoon salt

1/4 teaspoon pepper

4 green onions, diced

1 medium red pepper, diced

2 cloves garlic, minced

15-ounce can diced tomatoes

8-ounce can tomato sauce

1/2 cup red wine

1/2 teaspoon allspice

1/2 teaspoon thyme

1 bay leaf

1/8 teaspoon cayenne pepper

salt to taste

freshly ground black pepper to taste

In a large nonstick skillet heat oil. Add chicken breasts, sprinkle with salt and pepper, and fry over medium heat until brown on both sides. (Chicken does not have to be completely done at this point.) Remove chicken from pan and set aside on a plate. Add green onions, red pepper, and garlic. Cook for 2 minutes until onions are tender. Add diced tomatoes, tomato sauce, red wine, allspice, thyme, bay leaf, and cayenne pepper. Stir to mix well and bring to a boil. Add chicken back to pan, reduce heat, and partially cover pan. Simmer for 30 minutes or until chicken is completely done and sauce has reached desired consistency. Remove bay leaf. Add salt and pepper to taste. Serve with rice.

Serves 4

Nutrition Information per serving:
Calories: 270 – Fat: 9 gm. – Protein: 25 gm.
Carbohydrate: 22 gm. – Cholesterol: 50 mg. – Fiber: high

Chicken in Orange Pineapple Sauce with Dried Cranberries

 A tangy sauce with a hint of cinnamon makes this a beautiful chicken meal with lots of flavor. Great served with rice.

6 boneless, skinless chicken breast halves

1/2 cup flour

1 teaspoon salt

1 teaspoon freshly ground black pepper

2 tablespoons vegetable oil

6 ounces frozen orange juice concentrate

8 ounces crushed pineapple in juice

1/2 cup white wine

1/2 cup golden raisins

1/2 cup dried cranberries

1/4 teaspoon cinnamon

1/8 teaspoon ground cloves

1 teaspoon cornstarch

1 teaspoon sugar, optional

Preheat oven to 350°. Grease a 9 x 13 inch glass baking pan. Combine chicken in a plastic bag with flour, salt, and pepper. Toss to lightly coat chicken. In a heavy nonstick skillet, heat oil. Add chicken and fry until lightly browned on all sides. Place chicken in baking pan. Set aside.

In a small saucepan, combine orange juice concentrate, pineapple, wine, raisins, dried cranberries, cinnamon, cloves, and cornstarch. Bring to a boil, stirring constantly. Reduce heat and cook for 2 minutes. Add sugar if desired. Spoon half the sauce over chicken. Cover with aluminum foil. Bake for 30 to 40 minutes or until chicken is completely done. Check every 10 minutes and baste with extra sauce.

Serves 6

Nutrition Information per serving:
Calories: 355 – Fat: 7 gm. – Protein: 27 gm.
Carbohydrate: 46 gm. – Cholesterol: 50 mg. – Fiber: low

Chicken Marsala

 This is one of the more popular items ordered in restaurants. Make it at home quickly, and it tastes even better.

1/4 cup flour

1/4 cup grated Parmesan cheese

1/2 teaspoon black pepper

4 boneless, skinless chicken breast halves

1 tablespoon olive oil

1 pound fresh mushrooms, sliced

1/2 cup chicken stock

1 large bay leaf

1/2 cup Marsala wine

In a large plastic bag, mix flour, Parmesan cheese, and black pepper. Add chicken and toss well to coat. In a large skillet, heat oil to medium hot. Fry chicken until brown and thoroughly cooked. Remove chicken from pan. Set aside and keep warm. Add mushrooms, chicken stock, and bay leaf to the pan. Stir to deglaze pan and cook until mushrooms are tender. Add wine and cook over low heat until reduced by about one-half. Remove bay leaf. To serve, pour mushroom wine sauce over warm chicken.

Serves 4

Nutrition Information per serving:
Calories: 265 – Fat: 10 gm. – Protein: 32 gm.
Carbohydrate: 12 gm. – Cholesterol: 55 mg. – Fiber: low

Crab and Asparagus Quiche

 A special weekend treat. Prepare the egg mixture ahead of time and pour into a pie shell when ready to bake.

1/2 tablespoon butter or margarine	2/3 cup chicken broth
1/2 cup diced green onions	1/3 cup fat-free half-and-half
1/2 teaspoon basil	1/2 teaspoon salt
1/4 pound fresh asparagus, chopped and blanched	1/4 teaspoon cayenne pepper
	1 cup grated low-fat Swiss cheese, divided
1/2 pound crab or surimi	9-inch unbaked pie crust
3 eggs	1/4 teaspoon paprika

Preheat oven to 400°. In a medium skillet melt butter. Add onions and basil. Cook over medium heat until onions are translucent. Remove from heat. Add asparagus and crab. Set aside. In a medium bowl lightly beat eggs. Add chicken broth, half-and-half, salt, and pepper. Add asparagus and crab mixture to eggs. Add 1/2 cup of the Swiss cheese and stir gently. Pour into unbaked pie crust. Top with remaining 1/2 cup cheese. Sprinkle with paprika. Bake for 10 minutes. Reduce oven temperature to 325° and bake 30 minutes or until knife inserted in center comes out clean.

Note: Broccoli is a good substitute for asparagus in this quiche.

Serves 6

Nutritional Information per serving:
Calories: 260 – Fat: 13 gm. – Protein: 19 gm.
Carbohydrate: 16 gm. – Cholesterol: 130 mg. – Fiber: low

Curried Shrimp with Saffron Rice

 Garam masala curry powder is a blend of coriander, black pepper, cardamom, cinnamon, kalonji, caraway, cloves, ginger, and nutmeg. The extra turmeric will add the beautiful yellow color that is very good with vegetables, poultry, and fish.

2 tablespoons olive oil (divided)

1 teaspoon garam masala curry powder*

2 teaspoons hot curry powder or curry paste

1/2 teaspoon turmeric

1 pound shrimp, deveined

1 large onion, chopped

2 cloves garlic, minced

1 medium red pepper, chopped

1 medium green pepper, chopped, optional

16-ounce can tomatoes, chopped

1 medium zucchini, sliced

1/2 cup golden raisins

In a heavy skillet heat 1 tablespoon of the olive oil and add curry powders and turmeric. Cook, stirring constantly, for 1 minute. Add shrimp and cook over medium heat for 3 to 5 minutes or until shrimp are pink and cooked through. Remove shrimp from pan and set aside. Add remaining 1 tablespoon olive oil to pan. Add onions and cook over medium heat until translucent. Add garlic and peppers and cook for 1 minute. (Do not allow garlic to brown.) Add canned tomatoes, zucchini, and raisins. Bring to a boil. Reduce heat, cover, and simmer for 10 to 15 minutes. Add cooked shrimp and reheat. Serve over Saffron Rice (page 98).

*Note: In place of 1 teaspoon garam masala curry powder, substitute 1/4 teaspoon cinnamon, 1/4 teaspoon coriander, and 1/4 teaspoon cardamom.

Use the amount of curry powder and the type of curry powder to suit your taste.

Serves 4

Nutrition Information per serving without rice:
Calories: 290 – Fat: 9 gm. – Protein: 26 gm.
Carbohydrate: 26 gm. – Cholesterol: 170 mg. – Fiber: medium

Ginger Chicken

 An easy entree made special with ginger.

4 boneless, skinless chicken breast halves	1 tablespoon minced fresh ginger or
1/3 cup soy sauce	1 teaspoon ground ginger
2 tablespoons white wine vinegar	1/4 cup cooking oil
1 clove garlic, minced	1 tablespoon sesame oil

Place chicken breasts in resealable bag. In a small jar, mix soy sauce, vinegar, garlic, ginger, cooking oil, and sesame oil. Pour into bag with chicken. Mix well. Marinate in refrigerator for 30 minutes to several hours.

Remove chicken from marinade and grill over medium heat until chicken is brown and completely cooked. Cool and slice into thin diagonal slices.

Serves 4

Nutrition Information per serving:
Calories: 140 – Fat: 5 gm. – Protein: 22 gm.
Carbohydrate: 2 gm. – Cholesterol: 50 mg. – Fiber: low

Greek Turkey Pizza

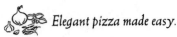 *Elegant pizza made easy.*

1 pound turkey tenderloin or turkey breast,
    cut into strips

1 large onion, sliced

2 tablespoons chopped fresh parsley

1 tablespoon fresh oregano or
    1 teaspoon dry oregano

1/2 teaspoon white pepper

1 tablespoon olive oil

2 tablespoons lemon zest

2 cloves garlic, minced

1 medium prebaked pizza crust

2 medium fresh tomatoes, seeded and
    chopped

12 large black olives, pitted and chopped

1/4 pound feta cheese, crumbled

Preheat oven to 450°. Lightly grease baking sheet. In a medium bowl combine turkey strips, onions, parsley, oregano, and white pepper. Mix well. In a medium frying pan, heat oil. Add seasoned turkey strips and onions and cook over medium heat for 5 to 7 minutes or until turkey is lightly browned. Turn heat to low and add lemon zest and garlic. Cook 1 minute. Set aside. Place pizza crust on baking sheet. Top with turkey mixture, tomatoes, olives, and cheese. Bake for 10 to 15 minutes or until heated through. Watch carefully to prevent burning. (The feta cheese does not actually melt.)

Serves 4

Nutrition Information per serving:
Calories: 465 – Fat: 20 gm. – Protein: 33 gm.
Carbohydrate: 38 gm. – Cholesterol: 90 mg. – Fiber: low

Grilled Salmon on a Bed of Lentils with Orange Lime Salsa

 An easy, attractive healthy meal. Thyme is the spice that makes it special.

Lentils:

1 tablespoon olive oil

1 small onion, finely chopped

3 cloves garlic, finely minced

1 cup lentils, washed

2 cups chicken broth

1/2 teaspoon dried thyme or
    1 teaspoon fresh thyme

1/2 teaspoon freshly ground pepper

1/2 cup grated carrots

1/4 cup finely chopped fresh parsley

salt and pepper to taste

Salmon:

1 1/2 pounds salmon fillet

salt and freshly ground pepper

2 tablespoons olive oil

1 tablespoon Dijon mustard

1 tablespoon lemon juice

1/2 teaspoon dried thyme or
    1 teaspoon fresh thyme

Heat grill. In a medium heavy skillet, heat oil and add onions. Cook until onions are translucent. Add garlic and cook 1 minute (do not brown). Add lentils, chicken broth, thyme, and pepper. Bring to a boil. Reduce heat and simmer, partially covered, for 30 to 40 minutes or until lentils are soft. Add grated carrots and parsley. Cook 10 to 15 minutes or until carrots are tender. Adjust seasoning with salt and pepper.

While lentils are cooking, sprinkle salmon with salt and pepper. In a small bowl, combine olive oil, mustard, lemon juice, and thyme. Brush mixture on salmon. Grill salmon over medium heat, turning only one time. Grill until lightly browned on the outside and completely done in the middle. Remove from grill and keep warm.

To serve, spoon lentils on serving plate and top with grilled salmon. Top salmon with Orange-Lime Salsa (see page 208).

Note: Salmon can also be fried in a small amount of oil over medium heat in a heavy, nonstick skillet.

Serves 4

Nutrition Information per serving:
Calories: 490 – Fat: 16 gm. – Protein: 53 gm.
Carbohydrate: 33 gm. – Cholesterol: 90 mg. – Fiber: very high

Honey-Basted Turkey Breast with Apricot-Pecan Dressing

 Turkey is a treat any time of the year. This recipe is fabulous with the allspice and honey basting on the turkey and the special dressing.

1 boneless turkey breast, about 3 pounds

Marinade:

1/2 cup white wine

2 tablespoons soy sauce

2 tablespoons lemon juice

1/2 teaspoon ground allspice

1 tablespoon honey

Dressing:

1 tablespoon butter

1 large onion, chopped

2 stalks celery, chopped

1/2 teaspoon rosemary, crushed

4 cups sage-and-onion-seasoned croutons

15 ounces low-fat chicken broth

1/2 cup pecans, chopped

1/2 cup dried apricots, diced

salt and pepper to taste

Place turkey breast in a large resealable plastic bag. Add wine, soy sauce, lemon juice, allspice, and honey. Mix well. Refrigerate several hours or overnight. Preheat oven to 325°. Grease a 7 x 11 inch baking pan or a 2-quart casserole dish. In a medium skillet, heat butter. Add onions, celery, and rosemary, and cook over medium heat until onions are translucent. Add croutons, broth, pecans, and apricots. Add salt and pepper to taste. Spoon dressing into pan. Remove turkey from marinade and place turkey on top of dressing. Cover loosely with aluminum foil. Bake for about 1 1/2 hours or until turkey temperature reaches 180°. While baking turkey, boil reserved marinade in a small saucepan until reduced to 1/3 cup. Baste turkey occasionally with reduced marinade. Remove foil toward the end of the baking period to brown the turkey.

Serves 6

Nutrition Information per serving:
Calories: 380 – Fat: 11 gm. – Protein: 40 gm.
Carbohydrate: 30 gm. – Cholesterol: 100 mg. – Fiber: low

Indonesian Marinated Chicken

 The coriander and cumin provide a wonderful, warm flavor to the chicken.

4 boneless, skinless chicken breast halves

2 tablespoons vegetable oil

2 tablespoons lemon juice

2 cloves garlic, minced

2 tablespoons soy sauce

2 teaspoons brown sugar

1 teaspoon ground coriander

1 teaspoon ground cumin

1/4 teaspoon cayenne pepper

1/8 teaspoon salt

1/2 cup white wine

1 tablespoon butter or margarine

Place chicken breasts in a large resealable plastic bag. In a small bowl or jar, combine all remaining ingredients except butter. Pour into bag and mix well with the chicken. Refrigerate for several hours.

When ready to serve, heat butter in medium nonstick skillet. Remove chicken from marinade; reserve marinade. Cook chicken, partially covered, over low-medium heat until brown on both sides. Add reserved marinade to deglaze pan and cook until reduced by half. Serve wine sauce on the side with chicken. Serve with Orange-Lime Salsa (page 208) or Peach and Apple Salsa (page 209).

Serves 4

Nutrition Information per serving:
Calories: 145 – Fat: 5 gm. – Protein: 21 gm.
Carbohydrate: 4 gm. – Cholesterol: 50 mg. – Fiber: 0

Lemon Mustard Chicken

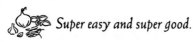 *Super easy and super good.*

3 tablespoons butter or margarine

4 boneless, skinless chicken breast halves

1/2 pound small whole fresh mushroom caps

1/4 cup Dijon mustard

1/4 cup fresh lemon juice

1 teaspoon dried tarragon

1 teaspoon salt

3/4 teaspoon freshly ground black pepper

1/4 teaspoon paprika

fresh tarragon or fresh parsley for garnish

Preheat oven to 350°. Grease 11 x 9 inch baking pan. In a medium skillet melt butter. Add chicken and brown quickly over medium heat. Remove from skillet and place in baking pan. (Chicken should not be cooked through at this point.) Add mushrooms to skillet and cook over medium heat until tender. Remove from heat and stir in mustard, lemon juice, tarragon, salt, and pepper. Spoon mixture over chicken. Bake chicken 30 to 45 minutes or until chicken is cooked thoroughly. Serve chicken topped with sauce. Sprinkle with paprika and garnish with fresh tarragon or fresh parsley.

Serves 4

Nutrition Information per serving:
Calories: 190 – Fat: 10 gm. – Protein: 22 gm.
Carbohydrate: 3 gm. – Cholesterol: 80 mg. – Fiber: 0

Oriental Pasta and Seafood

 An easy, attractive, and unusual recipe that can be prepared in less than 30 minutes. In place of surimi, choose shrimp or another seafood of your choice.

3/4 pound extra thin spaghetti

1 tablespoon peanut oil

1 medium onion, thinly sliced

1 medium red bell pepper, thinly sliced

1/2 pound fresh mushrooms, sliced

2 cloves garlic, minced

1/2 cup chicken broth

1/4 cup soy sauce

1/2 teaspoon crushed red pepper flakes

1/2 teaspoon ground ginger

4 cups shredded cabbage

1/2 pound surimi seafood

1/2 teaspoon freshly ground pepper or to taste

salt to taste

Cook spaghetti in boiling salted water until tender. Drain and set aside. In a large skillet heat oil. Cook onion over medium heat until translucent. Add peppers and mushrooms and cook until tender. Add garlic and cook 1 minute. Add chicken broth, soy sauce, red pepper flakes, ginger, and cabbage. Cook 4 to 5 minutes or until cabbage is wilted. Add surimi and cooked spaghetti to pan and mix gently to coat. Add freshly ground pepper. Cover skillet, reduce heat to low, and cook another 2 to 3 minutes or until surimi seafood is heated through. Add salt and extra red pepper flakes to taste.

Serves 4

Nutrition Information per serving:
Calories: 435 – Fat: 5 gm. – Protein: 22 gm.
Carbohydrate: 75 gm. – Cholesterol: 15 mg. – Fiber: medium

Savory Sea Bass

 A savory mixture of spices adds lots of flavor to a moist, mild fish.

1 1/2 pounds sea bass	1/4 teaspoon rosemary
1 egg white	1/4 teaspoon thyme
1/3 cup flour	1/4 teaspoon marjoram
1/4 cup freshly grated Parmesan cheese	1/2 teaspoon salt
1/2 teaspoon basil	1/2 teaspoon freshly ground pepper
1/4 teaspoon oregano	2 tablespoons cooking oil

Cut fish into 4 pieces. In a small bowl, lightly beat egg white. Set aside. In a shallow bowl combine flour, Parmesan cheese, basil, oregano, rosemary, thyme, marjoram, salt, and pepper. Dip fish into egg whites and then coat with flour mixture. In a large nonstick skillet, heat cooking oil. Fry fish over medium heat for 6 to 10 minutes on each side or until lightly browned and fish flakes easily when tested with a fork.

Serves 4

Nutrition Information per serving:
Calories: 260 – Fat: 7 gm. – Protein: 39 gm.
Carbohydrate: 9 gm. – Cholesterol: 65 mg. – Fiber: very low

Scallop Kabobs with Curry

 Serve as a dinner entree or in a smaller portion as an appetizer.

1 pound medium sea scallops

1 pint cherry tomatoes

1 medium green pepper, cut in chunks

1 medium red pepper, cut in chunks

1 cup pineapple chunks

1/3 cup lemon juice

2 tablespoons honey

2 tablespoons Dijon mustard

1 tablespoon vegetable oil

1 teaspoon curry powder

Alternate scallops, tomatoes, peppers, and pineapple on small wooden skewers. In a small bowl, combine lemon juice, honey, mustard, oil, and curry powder. Brush kabobs with sauce. Broil or grill until scallops are done, basting occasionally. Serve with extra sauce.

Serves 4

Nutrition Information per serving:
Calories: 250 – Fat: 5 gm. – Protein: 21 gm.
Carbohydrate: 30 gm. – Cholesterol: 35 mg. – Fiber: medium

Scallop Mushroom Bake

 A favorite of seafood lovers, but so easy. The thyme, rosemary, and pepper complement the scallops. This is elegant enough for a special company meal.

2 tablespoons butter or margarine

1 medium onion, finely chopped

1 pound fresh mushrooms, sliced

1 1/2 pounds sea scallops

1/2 cup white wine

1/2 teaspoon thyme

1/2 teaspoon rosemary, crushed

1/2 teaspoon freshly ground pepper

1/4 cup minced fresh parsley

3 tablespoons bread crumbs

3/4 cup grated Monterey Jack cheese

Preheat oven broiler. In a large nonstick skillet, melt butter. Over medium heat cook onions until translucent. Add mushrooms and cook until tender. Drain excess liquid from scallops. Add scallops, wine, thyme, rosemary, and pepper to skillet. Cook until scallops are thoroughly cooked. Remove scallops and mushrooms with a slotted spoon and distribute between 6 small individual baking dishes. Add parsley to the pan and continue to cook liquid in the pan until reduced to about 3/4 cup. Spoon 2 tablespoons of liquid over the scallops in each dish. Top each dish with 1/2 tablespoon of bread crumbs and 2 tablespoons grated cheese. Place individual dishes under oven broiler for about 5 minutes. Watch carefully. Broil until bread crumbs are brown and cheese is melted.

Note: This is a great company meal because it can be made ahead of time and refrigerated. Reheat in a 400° oven for 10 minutes and finish browning under the broiler.

Serves 6

Nutrition Information per serving:
Calories: 220 – Fat: 9 gm. – Protein: 25 gm.
Carbohydrate: 10 gm. – Cholesterol: 60 mg. – Fiber: low

Scallops with Linguine and Spinach

 An elegant meal done in less than 30 minutes. Also great with shrimp.

1 tablespoon olive oil

1 large onion, chopped

2 cloves garlic, minced

1/2 pound fresh mushrooms, sliced

1/4 teaspoon cayenne pepper

1/2 teaspoon salt

1 teaspoon basil

1/4 teaspoon thyme

1 large red bell pepper, thinly sliced

1/3 cup fresh lemon juice

1 tablespoon brown sugar

1 tablespoon lemon zest

1 pound fresh scallops or frozen scallops,
   thawed

1 cup low-fat chicken broth

2 tablespoons cornstarch

1/4 cup white wine

1/2 pound linguine

5 ounces (1/2 box) frozen spinach, chopped

freshly ground black pepper to taste

In a large heavy skillet, heat olive oil over medium heat. Add onions and cook until translucent. Add garlic and cook 1 minute. Add mushrooms, cayenne pepper, salt, basil, and thyme, and cook until mushrooms are tender. Add red bell pepper, lemon juice, brown sugar, lemon zest, and scallops. Cook uncovered over low heat for about 10 minutes or until scallops are thoroughly done. In a small custard cup, mix chicken broth with cornstarch. Add broth to scallop mixture, stirring constantly until mixture boils and thickens. Reduce heat and add wine. Hold over warm heat until ready to serve. While cooking scallops, cook pasta in salted boiling water. One minute before pasta is done, add spinach. Drain pasta and spinach and place in warm serving bowl. Pour scallop mixture on top. Sprinkle with freshly ground pepper.

Serves 4

Nutrition Information per serving:
Calories: 425 – Fat: 6 gm. – Protein: 32 gm.
Carbohydrate: 61 gm. – Cholesterol: 35 mg. – Fiber: high

Shrimp Tarragon

 This is so good! It has a delicate flavor that is from the tarragon and just a pinch of red and white pepper.

2 tablespoons butter

4 small green onions, chopped

1/4 teaspoon cayenne pepper

1/4 teaspoon white pepper

2 teaspoons dried tarragon

1/2 teaspoon paprika

1/4 teaspoon salt

1 pound fresh shrimp, peeled and deveined

1 pound fresh mushrooms, thickly sliced

1/2 cup low-fat chicken broth

1/2 cup white wine

In a large nonstick skillet, melt butter. In a small custard cup combine onions, cayenne pepper, white pepper, tarragon, paprika, and salt. Cook over medium heat, stirring constantly for 1 minute. Add shrimp and cook, stirring occasionally, until they turn pink. Add mushrooms, chicken broth, and wine. Continue cooking until mushrooms are tender and liquid is reduced by half. Serve over rice.

Serves 4

Nutrition Information per serving (without rice):
Calories: 240 – Fat: 8 gm. – Protein: 33 gm.
Carbohydrate: 9 gm. – Cholesterol: 200 mg. – Fiber: medium

Southern Comfort Chicken with Apricot Sauce

 This is a beautiful way to serve chicken. The blend of flavors is wonderful.

16-ounce can apricot halves in light syrup	4 boneless, skinless chicken breast halves
1 cup orange juice	1/4 cup flour
3 tablespoons cornstarch	1/2 teaspoon salt
1/4 cup Southern Comfort	1/4 teaspoon white pepper
1/2 teaspoon nutmeg	2 tablespoons vegetable oil

Preheat oven to 325°. Drain apricots, reserving syrup. Set apricots aside. In a small heavy saucepan, combine 1 cup of the apricot syrup, orange juice, and cornstarch. Stir until well mixed. Cook over medium-hot heat, stirring constantly, until mixture comes to a boil and thickens. Add Southern Comfort and nutmeg. Set aside. Place chicken breasts in plastic bag. Add flour, salt, and pepper. Shake until chicken is evenly covered. Heat oil over medium-hot heat in heavy skillet. Add chicken and fry until brown on both sides. Chicken does not have to be completely done at this point. Pour sauce over chicken, cover pan, and place in oven for 20 minutes or until chicken is cooked through. Remove cover and top with reserved apricot halves. Heat 5 minutes. Serve right from the pan or arrange on a platter.

Note: Brandy or apricot brandy can be substituted for the Southern Comfort.

Serves 4

Nutrition Information per serving:
Calories: 300 – Fat: 9 gm. – Protein: 28 gm.
Carbohydrate: 27 gm. – Cholesterol: 65 mg. – Fiber: medium

Spicy Cajun Shrimp

 Beautiful and delicious, but watch out. It can be as hot as you like it! Adjust the cayenne pepper and crushed red pepper to taste.

1 1/2 pounds shrimp, thawed and peeled

2 tablespoons butter or margarine

2 cloves garlic, minced

2 teaspoons Worcestershire sauce

1/2 teaspoon cayenne pepper

1/2 teaspoon freshly ground black pepper

1/2 teaspoon crushed red pepper

1 teaspoon basil, crushed

1/2 teaspoon thyme, crushed

2 medium tomatoes, seeded and chopped

1/2 cup beer, room temperature

Clean and devein shrimp under cold running water. Drain and set aside. In a large nonstick skillet, melt butter. Add garlic, Worcestershire sauce, cayenne pepper, black pepper, red pepper, basil, and thyme. Stir over medium heat 1 minute. Add shrimp. Cook until shrimp turn pink. Add tomatoes and beer. Cook for about 5 minutes or until liquid is reduced by half. Serve over rice.

Serves 4

Nutrition Information per serving (without rice):
Calories: 280 – Fat: 9 gm. – Protein: 45 gm.
Carbohydrate: 5 gm. – Cholesterol: 200 mg. – Fiber: low

Strawberry, Grape, and Turkey Salad

 Turkey is not just for Thanksgiving any more. Buy it already cooked or use leftover turkey for this recipe. It is a lovely salad with a lemon-orange flavored dressing. The touch of cinnamon and nutmeg makes it special.

1 pound cooked turkey breast, cut into cubes

1 cup fresh grapes

2 cups fresh strawberries, halved

lettuce leaves

Dressing:

8 ounces fat-free lemon yogurt

1 tablespoon orange juice concentrate

1 teaspoon orange zest

1/2 teaspoon cinnamon

1/4 teaspoon nutmeg

Spoon yogurt into fine strainer or coffee filter over a cup. Allow to drain for several hours in the refrigerator to remove excess liquid. Discard liquid. In a large bowl, combine turkey, grapes, and strawberries.

In a small bowl combine drained yogurt, orange juice concentrate, orange zest, cinnamon, and nutmeg. Add to turkey and fruit. Stir gently. Refrigerate until ready to serve. Serve on lettuce leaves.

Note: Other fresh or canned fruits can be used in this recipe.

Serves 6

Nutrition Information per serving:
Calories: 165 – Fat: 5 gm. – Protein: 17 gm.
Carbohydrate: 13 gm. – Cholesterol: 45 mg. – Fiber: low

Swordfish Steak with Lemon-Lime Marinade

 The combination of flavors in this marinade complements the mild swordfish.

2 pounds swordfish steaks

2 tablespoons lemon juice

2 tablespoons lime juice

2 tablespoons soy sauce

2 tablespoons honey

1 tablespoon Dijon mustard

1/4 cup vegetable oil

2 teaspoons dill weed

1/4 teaspoon cayenne pepper

1/2 teaspoon salt

Cut swordfish into four pieces. Place in resealable plastic bag. In a small jar combine lemon juice, lime juice, soy sauce, honey, mustard, oil, dill weed, pepper, and salt. Mix well and pour into bag with swordfish. Reseal and refrigerate several hours. When ready to serve, heat grill to medium-hot. Remove fish from bag and grill until lightly browned on both sides and fish flakes easily.

Note: In place of grilling, the swordfish can be fried in a small amount of oil in a nonstick skillet. Fry over medium heat. Watch carefully to prevent burning.

Serve with Orange-Lime Salsa (page 208) or Peach and Apple Salsa (page 209).

Serves 4

Nutrition Information per serving:
Calories: 315 – Fat: 12 gm. – Protein: 45 gm.
Carbohydrate: 6 gm. – Cholesterol: 90 mg. – Fiber: very low

Turkey Cutlets in White Wine Sauce

 Take advantage of buying your favorite parts of turkey without the hassle of preparing a whole turkey. This recipe is a delightful treat. Lightly browned slices of turkey breast in a light wine gravy and served with tangy fresh cranberry salsa.

1/3 cup flour	1 tablespoon vegetable oil
1/2 teaspoon marjoram, crushed	2 tablespoons cornstarch
1/4 teaspoon thyme	1 cup chicken broth
1/4 teaspoon white pepper	1/2 cup white wine
1/2 teaspoon salt	salt and pepper to taste
1 1/2 pounds thinly sliced turkey breast	

Combine flour, marjoram, thyme, white pepper, and salt in a medium plastic bag. Add turkey cutlets and toss until well coated. In a large, heavy non-stick skillet, heat oil. Add cutlets, and fry over medium-hot heat until brown and thoroughly done. Remove turkey and set aside on a plate and keep warm. Stir cornstarch into chicken broth and add to frying pan. Cook, stirring constantly, until mixture boils and thickens. Add wine, and heat. If sauce is too thick add extra chicken broth. Adjust seasoning with salt and pepper to taste. To serve, spoon wine sauce over turkey cutlets.

Serve with Cranberry and Roasted Pepper Salsa (page 204).

Serves 4

Nutrition Information per serving:
Calories: 265 – Fat: 6 gm. – Protein: 42 gm.
Carbohydrate: 10 gm. – Cholesterol: 70 mg. – Fiber: low

Turkey Medallions with Apricot Chutney

 Turkey any time of the year with a warm fruit chutney and a touch of brandy.

Chutney:

1 cup dried apricots, coarsely chopped

1/2 cup golden raisins

1/3 cup cider vinegar

1 cup water

1/2 teaspoon cinnamon

1/2 teaspoon ground ginger

1/4 teaspoon nutmeg

1/4 teaspoon ground cloves

1 teaspoon dry mustard

1/4 teaspoon red pepper flakes, optional

1 large apple, peeled and chopped

Turkey:

1 pound turkey breast medallions,
    3/4-inch thick

1/2 teaspoon salt

1/2 teaspoon freshly ground pepper

1 tablespoon butter or margarine

2 tablespoons brandy

In a large heavy saucepan, combine apricots, raisins, vinegar, water, cinnamon, ginger, nutmeg, cloves, dry mustard, and red pepper flakes. Bring to a boil, stirring constantly. Reduce heat, cover, and simmer for 20 minutes. Stir occasionally. Add apple; cover and cook another 15 minutes or until apple is tender. Remove from heat and uncover. Set aside.

Sprinkle turkey medallions with salt and pepper. In a heavy frying pan over medium heat, melt butter. Add turkey and fry until light brown and cooked thoroughly. Add brandy and stir until pan is deglazed. To serve, spoon warm chutney over turkey medallions. Refrigerate any leftover chutney.

Serves 4

Nutrition Information per serving:
Calories: 340 – Fat: 5 gm. – Protein: 28 gm.
Carbohydrate: 46 gm. – Cholesterol: 55 mg. – Fiber: medium

West Indian Saffron Shrimp

 If you like the exotic taste of Indian cuisine you will love this shrimp dish. It is quick and easy—done in 15 minutes.

1 medium pinch saffron threads
   (about 35 threads)

2 tablespoons peanut oil

1/2 cup green onions, finely chopped

1/4 teaspoon marjoram

1/4 teaspoon thyme

1/2 teaspoon cumin

1 1/2 pounds shrimp, peeled and deveined

2 teaspoons angostura bitters

1/4 cup red wine

In a small custard cup combine saffron threads with 2 teaspoons warm water. Set aside. In a medium nonstick skillet, heat oil over medium heat. In a small custard cup combine onions, marjoram, thyme, and cumin. Add to skillet and cook for 1 minute, stirring constantly. Add shrimp and saffron. Cook until shrimp is pink and thoroughly done. Stir in bitters and red wine. Heat through. Serve on rice.

Serves 4

Nutrition Information per serving (without rice):
Calories: 300 – Fat: 11 gm. – Protein: 46 gm.
Carbohydrate: 4 gm. – Cholesterol: 250 mg. – Fiber: very low

Sauces and Salsas

Apple-Cranberry Sauce

 A zesty accompaniment for poultry and pork.

3/4 cup water

1/2 cup sugar

1/2 teaspoon allspice

1 tablespoon lemon juice

4 cups peeled and diced apples

2 cups fresh or frozen cranberries,
  washed and sorted

Combine water, sugar, allspice, and lemon juice in a medium saucepan. Bring to a boil, and stir until sugar is dissolved. Add apples and cranberries. Reduce heat and simmer, partially covered, for 20 minutes or until apples are tender and cranberries have popped. The sauce thickens as it cools.

Serves 8

Nutrition Information per serving:
Calories: 90 – Fat: 0 gm. – Protein: 23
Carbohydrate: 0 gm. – Cholesterol: 0 mg. – Fiber: medium

Black Bean Salsa

 Make it hot or make it mild. The cilantro and chile pepper give this salsa a southwestern flavor. Serve with corn chips.

15-ounce can black beans, rinsed and
    drained
1 large tomato, seeded and chopped
1/2 cup frozen corn
1/2 cup minced onions
1/4 cup fresh minced cilantro
1 small hot chile pepper, seeded and
    finely chopped

1 clove garlic, minced
1 tablespoon lime juice
1 tablespoon olive oil
1/4 teaspoon cayenne pepper
1/4 teaspoon freshly ground pepper
salt to taste

In a large bowl combine all ingredients. Cover and refrigerate several hours to blend flavors.

Serves 6

Nutrition Information per serving:
Calories: 105 – Fat: 2 gm. – Protein: 5 gm.
Carbohydrate: 17 gm. – Cholesterol: 0 mg. – Fiber: high

Blue Cheese Dressing

 I love blue cheese dressing but usually make myself avoid it because it is so high in calories and fat. With this recipe I can have my dressing without any guilt and it tastes fantastic. The mustard powder and white pepper are essential.

1/4 teaspoon dry mustard

4 ounces blue cheese, crumbled

1 cup fat-free mayonnaise

1 cup fat-free sour cream

2 cloves garlic, finely minced

1/8 teaspoon white pepper

2–4 tablespoons buttermilk

salt and freshly ground pepper to taste

In a small custard cup combine dry mustard with 1 teaspoon cool water. In a small bowl combine blue cheese, mayonnaise, sour cream, garlic, white pepper, and mustard. Add buttermilk to make the desired consistency. Add salt and pepper to taste.

Serves 12 (3 tablespoons per serving)

Nutrition Information per serving:
Calories: 65 – Fat: 3 gm. – Protein: 3 gm.
Carbohydrate: 6 gm. – Cholesterol: 10 mg. – Fiber: 0

Blueberry Sauce

 So good served over frozen yogurt, ice cream, cake, pancakes, or waffles.

1/3 cup brown sugar

1 tablespoon cornstarch

1/2 teaspoon cinnamon

1/8 teaspoon cloves

1/8 teaspoon nutmeg

1/4 cup water

1/4 cup fresh lemon juice

2 teaspoons lemon zest

3 cups (1 pound) fresh or loose-packed
    frozen blueberries

In a medium saucepan, combine brown sugar, cornstarch, cinnamon, cloves, and nutmeg. Add water, lemon juice, and lemon zest. Mix well. Place over medium heat and cook, stirring constantly, until mixture comes to a boil and thickens. Reduce heat and add blueberries. Simmer just until blueberries are warm. Remove from heat and serve warm.

Serves 8

Nutrition Information per serving:
Calories: 60 – Fat: 0 gm. – Protein: 0 gm.
Carbohydrate: 15 gm. – Cholesterol: 0 mg. – Fiber: medium

Cocktail Sauce

 Serve with fish or seafood for lots of zip and very few calories.

1 1/2 cups catsup

1 tablespoon prepared horseradish

1 teaspoon Worcestershire sauce

1/2 teaspoon dry mustard

2 drops hot pepper sauce

Mix all ingredients and refrigerate in covered jar.

Serves 8

Nutrition Information per serving:
Calories: 50 – Fat: 0 gm. – Protein: 1 gm.
Carbohydrate: 12 gm. – Cholesterol: 0 mg. – Fiber: very low

Corn, Peppers, and Tomato Salsa

 Attractive and lots of taste. Add crushed red pepper
if you like a few beads of perspiration on your neck.

10 ounces frozen corn

1/2 cup finely chopped red onions

1/2 medium red bell pepper, chopped

1/2 medium green bell pepper, chopped

4 medium fresh tomatoes, seeded and
    chopped

1 clove garlic, minced

2 tablespoons lime juice

1 tablespoon olive oil

1/2 teaspoon ground coriander

1/4 teaspoon ground cumin

1/4 teaspoon cayenne pepper

1/2 teaspoon salt

1/2 teaspoon sugar

crushed red pepper to taste

Combine all ingredients in a large bowl. Cover and refrigerate several hours to blend flavors. Taste and adjust seasoning with extra salt, sugar, or pepper as desired.

Serves 8

Nutrition Information per serving:
Calories: 75 – Fat: 2 gm. – Protein: 2 gm.
Carbohydrate: 12 gm. – Cholesterol: 0 mg. – Fiber: medium

Cranberry and Roasted Pepper Salsa

 This is one of those keeper recipes. Once you taste it you will want to keep it on hand. Attractive red salsa with roasted peppers, cilantro, and orange zest. Serve with pork or poultry.

2 red peppers, roasted, peeled and diced*

3 cups fresh cranberries (12 ounces)

1/4 cup fresh orange juice

2 tablespoons lime juice

2/3 cup sugar

1/3 cup cilantro leaves

1 tablespoon orange zest

Roast peppers under broiler or over open flame until skin is blistered and black. Place peppers in brown bag for 5 minutes to steam briefly. Peel black skin from peppers, and discard skin. Dice peppers. Set aside. Blend cranberries, orange juice, lime juice, sugar, and cilantro leaves in a food processor. Process just until cranberries are finely chopped. Add peppers and process briefly. Transfer to a bowl and mix in orange zest. Makes 2 1/2 cups. (Serving size 3 tablespoons.)

*Note: Ready-to-serve roasted peppers are available in jars. Substitute 3 1/2 ounces or 1/2 cup chopped canned peppers for the 2 fresh peppers.

Serves 12

Nutrition Information per serving:
Calories: 65 – Fat: 0 gm. – Protein: 0 gm.
Carbohydrate: 16 gm. – Cholesterol: 0 mg. – Fiber: medium

Creamy Garlic Peppercorn Dressing

 A healthy zesty dressing that tastes great on lettuce salads or on fresh tomato salads. You won't believe it can be so good and be made from tofu.

1 cup soft tofu

1 cup fat-free sour cream

2 cloves garlic, minced

1/4 cup grated Parmesan cheese

2 tablespoons fresh lemon juice

1 teaspoon lemon zest

1 teaspoon freshly ground pepper

1 teaspoon sugar

salt to taste

Combine all ingredients except salt in a food processor. Blend until smooth. Add salt to taste. Store in the refrigerator. Keeps well for about 2 weeks.

Makes 2 cups

Nutrition Information per tablespoon:
Calories: 16 – Fat: 0.5 gm. – Protein: 1 gm.
Carbohydrate: 2 gm. – Cholesterol: 2 mg. – Fiber: very low

Curry Sauce

 A spicy sauce to use as a dip for fresh vegetables or a dressing for salad greens. This also makes a zesty sandwich spread when used to prepare tuna salad.

1–2 teaspoons hot or sweet curry powder (to suit your taste)	1 cup fat-free sour cream
	2 green onions, chopped
1 tablespoon water	1/4 tablespoon garlic powder, optional

In a small bowl, mix curry powder and water. Add sour cream, onions, and garlic powder. Mix well. Store in covered container in the refrigerator.

Note: Choose the curry that suits your taste. You may want to start with 1/2 teaspoon and add more if you would like a more intense flavor.

Serves 8

Nutrition Information per serving:
Calories: 20 – Fat: 0 gm. – Protein: 1 gm.
Carbohydrate: 3 gm. – Cholesterol: 0 mg. – Fiber: very low

Fresh Tomato Salsa

 Healthy, low calorie, and lots of flavor. The fresh cilantro is essential.

3 medium fresh tomatoes, seeded and
    chopped
1 medium sweet onion, finely chopped
1 clove garlic, minced
1 small jalapeño pepper, seeded and minced

1/4 cup minced fresh cilantro
1 tablespoon minced fresh oregano
2 tablespoons lemon juice
1 tablespoon olive oil

Combine all ingredients and refrigerate in a covered bowl or jar.

Serves 4

Nutrition Information per serving:
Calories: 65 – Fat: 3 gm. – Protein: 1 gm.
Carbohydrate: 8 gm. – Cholesterol: 0 mg. – Fiber: medium

Orange-Lime Salsa

 Especially good served with grilled fish or pork. Be careful with the jalapeño.

3 medium oranges

1/2 small red onion, finely chopped

1 small jalapeño pepper, finely chopped

1/2 cup finely chopped fresh parsley

2 tablespoons fresh lime juice

1/4 teaspoon freshly ground pepper

1/4 teaspoon salt

Peel oranges and separate the sections. Remove and discard the membrane. Chop orange sections into small pieces. In a small bowl combine oranges with onion, jalapeño pepper, parsley, lime juice, pepper, and salt. Cover and refrigerate until ready to serve.

Serves 4

Nutritional Information:
Calories: 90 – Fat: 0 gm. – Protein: 2 gm.
Carbohydrate: 21 gm. – Cholesterol: 0 mg. – Fiber: high

Peach and Apple Salsa

 Honey, lime, and cilantro with a touch of allspice.
Great served with poultry or fish.

3 medium fresh peaches, peeled and diced

1 medium Granny Smith apple, peeled and
diced

1/4 cup chopped fresh cilantro

1/4 cup honey

2 tablespoons fresh lime juice

1/4 teaspoon allspice

1/4 teaspoon cinnamon

In a small bowl, combine all ingredients. Cover and refrigerate until ready
to use. Best when used the same day.

Serves 4

Nutrition Information per serving:
Calories: 115 – Fat 0: gm. – Protein: 1 gm.
Carbohydrate: 28 – Cholesterol: 0 mg. – Fiber: low

Prune Purée

 Prune purée can be used in some recipes as a replacement for part of the fat or oil.

1 1/3 cups (8 ounces) pitted prunes   1/2 cup water

Combine prunes and water in a food processor. Pulse on and off until prunes are finely chopped and smooth. Makes 1 cup.

Note: Prune purée and other fruit purees can be purchased in the baking section of your supermarket. They are fat free and have approximately 35 calories per tablespoon. Some brands may be more diluted with water and this will change the baking properties.

The key to a moist, tender product when preparing baked goods is reducing fat, not completely eliminating all fat. Experiment with your recipes. Start by cutting the fat in half and replacing that amount with fruit purée.

Serves 16

Nutrition Information per tablespoon:
Calories: 35 – Fat: 0 gm. – Protein: 0.5 gm.
Carbohydrate: 8 gm. – Cholesterol: 0 mg. – Fiber: high

Rhubarb Apricot Chutney

The word chutney *comes from the East Indian word* chatni. *This spicy condiment is made from fruit, vinegar, sugar, and spices. It can range in texture from chunky to smooth and in degrees of spiciness from mild to hot. Chutney adds interest to meats and entrees. Some chutney varieties make interesting bread spreads and are delicious when served with cheese. This chutney is good served with chicken or pork.*

2 cups diced rhubarb, fresh or frozen

2 cups dried apricot halves, diced

1 small red onion, minced

1 cup honey

1 cup golden raisins

2 cups cider vinegar

2 tablespoons lemon juice

1 tablespoon lemon zest

1 tablespoon minced gingerroot or

    1/2 teaspoon ground ginger

1 teaspoon allspice

1/2 teaspoon cloves

1 teaspoon cinnamon

1/4 teaspoon cayenne pepper, optional

In a heavy saucepan, combine all ingredients. Bring to a boil; reduce heat, cover, and simmer for 20 to 30 minutes. Serve warm or cold. Store in the refrigerator.

Serves 8

Nutrition Information per serving:
Calories: 315 – Fat: 0 gm. – Protein: 2 gm.
Carbohydrate: 77 gm. – Cholesterol: 0 mg. – Fiber: high

Seasoned Butters

 Mix any favorite seasonings into butter to add a flavor treat to breads, pastas, and vegetables.

1/4 pound butter or margarine, softened

Tarragon Butter: add 1 tablespoon tarragon and 1 tablespoon Dijon mustard

Peppery Butter: add 1 tablespoon dry mustard, 1 teaspoon freshly ground pepper, and 1/4 teaspoon cayenne pepper

Italian Herb Butter: add 1/2 teaspoon oregano, 1/4 teaspoon thyme, 1/4 teaspoon marjoram, and 1/4 teaspoon rosemary

Garlic Butter: add 1/2 teaspoon paprika, 2 cloves minced garlic, and 1/4 teaspoon white pepper

Lemon Butter: add 2 tablespoons lemon juice, 1 teaspoon Worcestershire sauce, and 2 teaspoons lemon zest

Cinnamon-Sugar Butter: add 1 teaspoon cinnamon, 1/4 teaspoon nutmeg, and 1 tablespoon sugar

Serves 8

Nutrition Information per tablespoon:
Calories: 100 – Fat: 11 – Protein: 0 gm.
Carbohydrate: 0 gm. – Cholesterol: 30 mg. – Fiber: very low

Strawberry Breakfast Salsa

 Serve with pancakes, waffles, or French toast.
Also great combined with vanilla yogurt.

1/2 cup apricot jam

1/4 cup water

1/2 teaspoon cinnamon

1/4 teaspoon allspice

4 cups fresh strawberries, hulled and sliced

In a large bowl, stir together jam, water, cinnamon, and allspice. Add strawberries and stir gently. Cover bowl and refrigerate.

Serves 4

Nutrition Information per serving:
Calories: 145 — Fat: 0 gm. — Protein: 1 gm.
Carbohydrate: 35 gm. — Cholesterol: 0 mg. — Fiber: high

Tartar Sauce

 Seasonings can make the fat-free mayonnaise taste almost as good as the high-fat mayo. This recipe has only 11 calories per tablespoon compared to regular tartar sauce with 100 calories per tablespoon.

1 1/2 cups fat-free mayonnaise

1/4 cup pickle relish or finely chopped
   dill pickle

2 green onions, finely chopped

1 tablespoon finely chopped fresh parsley

1/2 teaspoon tarragon

1/4 teaspoon cayenne pepper

1/2 teaspoon dry mustard

1 teaspoon tarragon vinegar or lemon juice

salt and extra pepper to taste

Mix all ingredients. Adjust seasonings to taste. Refrigerate in covered jar.

Serves 8

Nutrition Information per serving:
Calories: 35 – Fat: 0 gm. – Protein: 0 gm.
Carbohydrate: 9 gm. – Cholesterol: 0 mg. – Fiber: very low

Tomato Onion Chutney

 Serve with chicken, pork, or curry dishes.

3 cups chopped onions

1 teaspoon yellow mustard seeds
   or mustard powder

2 tablespoons butter or margarine

6 medium tomatoes, peeled, seeded,
   and diced

1 tablespoon red wine vinegar

1 tablespoon sugar

1/8 teaspoon allspice

1 pinch cayenne pepper

1 pinch mace (optional)

1 tablespoon minced fresh parsley

salt and pepper to taste

In a medium frying pan, cook onions and mustard seeds in butter over medium heat until onions are translucent. Add tomatoes, vinegar, sugar, allspice, pepper, and mace. Cook for 20 to 25 minutes until chutney is thick. Add parsley. Add salt and pepper to taste.

Note: A 15-ounce can of diced tomatoes can be substituted for the fresh tomatoes.

Serves 4

Nutrition Information per serving:
Calories: 100 – Fat: 3 gm. – Protein: 2 gm.
Carbohydrate: 16 gm. – Cholesterol: 15 mg. – Fiber: high

Desserts

Apple Cake with Hot Buttered Rum Sauce

 A real homemade cake with apples and apple pie spices served with a warm brown sugar rum sauce.

1/4 cup butter

1 cup sugar

1 egg

1/2 teaspoon salt

1 teaspoon baking soda

1/2 teaspoon cinnamon

1/4 teaspoon ginger

1/4 teaspoon nutmeg

1 teaspoon vanilla

1 cup flour

2 cups peeled and finely diced apples

1/2 cup walnuts, chopped

Topping:

1/4 cup evaporated milk

2 tablespoons butter or margarine

1/2 cup brown sugar

1 tablespoon rum

Preheat oven to 325°. Butter a 7 x 11 inch baking pan. In a large bowl beat butter and sugar until creamy. Add egg and beat until smooth. Add salt, baking soda, cinnamon, ginger, nutmeg, and vanilla. Beat until well mixed. Stir in flour and mix just until smooth. Stir in apples and nuts. Pour into pan. Bake for 25 to 30 minutes or until cake is done. The cake should be lightly browned and the middle of cake should spring back when touched lightly with your finger.

Prepare topping: In a small saucepan combine evaporated milk, butter, and brown sugar. Stir over medium heat until mixture just comes to a boil. Immediately remove from heat. (Mixture will curdle if allowed to boil rapidly.) Add rum. Serve warm over individual pieces of cake.

Note: To use a 9 x 13 inch pan, prepare 1 1/2 times the recipe.

Serves 10

Nutrition Information per serving:
Calories: 250 – Fat: 9 gm. – Protein: 2 gm.
Carbohydrate: 40 gm. – Cholesterol: 35 mg. – Fiber: low

Apple Raspberry Cobbler

When I serve this dessert, guests ask for seconds. My husband claims it is addictive. He even eats it for breakfast. The recipe is large enough to make one pan for your family and one to share at work. It could keep for a week in the refrigerator, but unless I hide it, it never lasts that long.

8 medium cooking apples, such as Cortland, peeled and sliced

4 cups raspberries, fresh or frozen loose pack in a bag

0.6 ounce package raspberry flavored, sugar-free gelatin powder (or 2 0.3-ounce packages)

2 tablespoons sugar

1 teaspoon cinnamon

1 teaspoon nutmeg

1 box (18.25 ounces) yellow cake mix

1/2 cup butter or stick margarine, cold

1 1/2 cups water

Preheat oven to 325°. Butter two 7 x 11 inch or two 9 x 9 inch pans or one 10 x 14 inch baking pan. Place apple slices on the bottom of the pan(s). Distribute raspberries evenly on top of apples. In a small custard cup combine gelatin powder, sugar, cinnamon, and nutmeg. Sprinkle gelatin mixture evenly over fruit. Set aside. Pour dry cake mix into a small bowl. Add butter and cut into dry mix with a knife or pastry blender until mixture resembles coarse cornmeal. Spoon dry mix evenly over fruit in the baking pan. Smooth with a knife. Pour water evenly over the dry mix in the pan. Bake for 45 to 50 minutes or until bottom is bubbly and top is lightly browned. Cool for an hour before serving. Serve at room temperature or chilled.

Note: The correct pan size is important for this recipe. The recipe does not work well in one 9 x 13 inch pan. Note the pan size options.

Serves 16

Nutrition Information per serving:
Calories: 275 – Fat: 9 gm. – Protein: 7 gm.
Carbohydrate: 41 mg. – Fiber: medium

Apricot and Cranberry Compote

Attractive, appetizing hot fruit with a tangy taste. Make ahead and keep refrigerated. Warm it up in the microwave when ready to serve. Serve on ice cream, frozen yogurt, or pound cake, or try it on cereal for breakfast.

1 1/2 cups dried apricot halves, cut in half

12 ounces frozen raspberry lemonade concentrate, thawed

2 tablespoons cornstarch

2 tablespoons honey

1/2 teaspoon allspice

1/8 teaspoon cardamom

2 cups fresh or frozen cranberries, washed and sorted

1 large apple, peeled, cored, and diced

Preheat oven to 325°. In a small saucepan cover apricots with water. Bring to a boil. Cover pan and remove from heat. Let stand for 15 minutes. Drain. In a medium 1 1/2 quart oven-proof bowl combine lemonade concentrate, cornstarch, honey, allspice, and cardamom. Stir until well mixed. Add cranberries, apples, and drained apricots. Stir. Cover and bake for 50 to 60 minutes or until mixture thickens and cranberries and apricots are tender. Mixture will continue to thicken as it cools.

Serves 10

Nutrition Information per serving:
Calories: 160 – Fat: 0 gm. – Protein: 1 gm.
Carbohydrate: 39 gm. – Cholesterol: 0 mg. – Fiber: high

Badger State Chocolate Cake

 This recipe was adapted from a popular old high-fat recipe often called Texas Sheet Cake. It is a chocolate lover's dream come true—so rich tasting, yet so low in fat. Be sure to use real vanilla. Enjoy without guilt!

2 cups sugar

1/2 cup shortening

2 eggs

1/3 cup unsweetened cocoa

2 teaspoons baking soda

1/2 teaspoon salt

2 teaspoons vanilla extract

6-ounce jar baby food apricots or
   3/4 cup prune purée*

1/2 cup coffee

2 cups flour

1/2 cup plain low-fat yogurt

Frosting:

3 cups powdered sugar

2 tablespoons butter or margarine

1/4 cup evaporated fat-free milk

1/3 cup unsweetened cocoa

3 ounces low-fat cream cheese

1 teaspoon vanilla extract

3/4 cup pecans, chopped

Preheat oven to 350°. Spray an 11 x 18 inch or 10 x 15 inch sheet-cake pan with nonstick vegetable oil spray. For a thinner cake choose the larger pan. In a large bowl, beat together sugar and shortening. Add eggs and beat well. Add cocoa, baking soda, and salt. Stir gently to prevent cocoa from flying out of the bowl. Add vanilla, apricots, and coffee. Beat until smooth. Stir in flour. Stir in yogurt. Spread batter in baking pan. Bake for 20 minutes for the larger pan or 25 to 30 minutes for the smaller pan, or until a wooden pick inserted in the middle of the cake comes out clean. Let cool in the pan.

Frosting: Place powdered sugar in a large bowl. Set aside. In a small saucepan combine butter and milk. Heat until butter is melted. Stir in cocoa and stir constantly over low heat until smooth. Add cocoa mixture to powdered sugar and beat with an electric mixer until smooth. Add cream cheese and vanilla. Beat until smooth. Stir in nuts. If frosting is too thick, add extra milk, 1 teaspoon at a time. Immediately spread over the cake. (Note: This cake freezes well.)

*Note: To make your own prune purée see recipe on page 210.

Serves 24

Nutrition Information per serving:
Calories: 250 – Fat: 7 gm. – Protein: 3 gm.
Carbohydrate: 43 gm. – Cholesterol: 20 mg. – Fiber: medium

Blond Brownies with Cranberries and Walnuts

If you like it sweet with a tease of tart, you will love these bars.

1/2 cup butter-flavored shortening

1 cup sugar

1 cup brown sugar

2 eggs

2 tablespoons orange liqueur

1 1/2 cups flour

2 teaspoons baking powder

1/2 teaspoon salt

1/2 teaspoon allspice

1 cup chopped cranberries

1/2 cup toasted chopped walnuts

Preheat oven to 350°. Butter a 9 x 11 inch baking pan. In a medium bowl beat shortening, sugar, and brown sugar until light. Add eggs and orange liqueur. Beat well. Stir in flour, baking powder, salt, and allspice. Stir in cranberries and walnuts. Spoon into baking pan. Bake for 20 to 30 minutes or until light brown on top.

Serves 16

Nutrition Information per serving:
Calories: 200 – Fat: 7 gm. – Protein: 2 gm.
Carbohydrate: 32 gm. – Cholesterol: 20 mg. – Fiber: very low

Blueberry Apple Crumble

 This tastes as good as blueberry apple pie but it can be made without a high-fat crust.

4 medium cooking apples such as Cortlands,
   cored, peeled, and sliced

1 1/2 cups frozen or fresh blueberries

1 tablespoon lemon juice

1/2 cup sugar

1/2 teaspoon cinnamon

1/4 teaspoon nutmeg

1/4 teaspoon allspice

9-inch unbaked pie crust (optional)

Topping:

1/4 cup flour

1/4 cup brown sugar

1/8 teaspoon nutmeg

2 tablespoons butter

freshly grated nutmeg

Preheat oven to 425°. Butter heavily the bottom and sides of a nonstick 9-inch pie pan or an 8 x 8 inch square nonstick baking pan. In a large bowl combine apples, blueberries, and lemon juice. In a small custard cup combine sugar, cinnamon, nutmeg, and allspice. Mix gently with the apples and berries. Spoon into baking pan or unbaked pie crust. For topping, combine flour, brown sugar, and nutmeg in a small bowl. Cut in butter. Sprinkle over apples and berries. Bake for 10 minutes. Reduce oven temperature to 325° and bake for 40 to 50 minutes or until apples are tender. Spoon into dessert bowls and serve warm with ice cream or frozen yogurt. Top with extra freshly grated nutmeg.

Serves 6

Nutrition Information per serving without crust:
Calories: 200 – Fat: 4 gm. – Protein: 1 gm.
Carbohydrate: 42 gm. – Cholesterol: 10 mg. – Fiber: high

Blueberry Gelatin Pie

 A way to include the antioxidants found in grape juice and blueberries in a refreshing, lovely dessert.

3-ounce package lemon-flavored gelatin
    powder

1/2 cup water

2 tablespoons cornstarch

1 cup grape juice

1 tablespoon lemon juice

1/2 teaspoon nutmeg

4 cups fresh blueberries, washed

9-inch baked pie crust

In a small saucepan, mix gelatin powder with water. Cook over medium heat, stirring constantly until gelatin is completely dissolved. In a small jar or glass, mix cornstarch with grape juice. Add to gelatin. Bring to a boil, stirring constantly until mixture has thickened and appears clear. Stir in lemon juice and nutmeg. Set aside until mixture cools to close to room temperature. Add blueberries and stir gently. Pour mixture into prebaked pie crust. Refrigerate until firm.

Note: To reduce the calories, omit the pie crust. Pour blueberry mixture directly into the pie pan. Refrigerate until firm.

Serves 8

Nutrition Information per serving with the crust:
Calories: 210 – Fat: 6 gm. – Protein: 3 gm.
Carbohydrate: 36 – Cholesterol: 0 mg. – Fiber: medium

Nutrition Information per serving without the crust:
Calories: 110 – Fat: 0 gm. – Protein: 1 gm.
Carbohydrate: 26 gm. – Cholesterol: 0 mg. – Fiber: medium

Caramel Cheesecake

 This may be the smoothest, best tasting cheesecake you have ever made.

1 cup graham cracker crumbs

1/4 cup sugar

3 tablespoons butter or margarine, melted

8 ounces Neufchatel cheese, room
  temperature

4 ounces fat-free cream cheese, room
  temperature

1/2 cup caramel ice cream topping

3 eggs

2 tablespoons fat-free milk

2 teaspoons vanilla

Topping:

1/2 cup fat-free sour cream

1/4 cup caramel ice cream topping

1/4 cup pecans, finely chopped

Preheat oven to 325°. In an 8-inch pie pan, combine graham cracker crumbs with sugar and melted butter. Mix with a fork. Press crumbs firmly in bottom of the pan and up the sides. Set aside. In a medium bowl beat Neufchatel cheese, cream cheese, and 1/2 cup caramel topping with an electric beater. Add eggs, milk, and vanilla. Beat until smooth. Pour filling into crust. Bake for 40 to 50 minutes or until light golden. Cool in pan for 30 minutes. In a small bowl combine sour cream and 1/4 cup caramel topping. Spread on baked cheesecake. Sprinkle with chopped pecans. Chill in refrigerator.

Serves 8

Nutrition Information per serving:
Calories: 325 – Fat: 15 gm. – Protein: 9 gm.
Carbohydrate: 39 gm. – Cholesterol: 100 mg. – Fiber: very low

Cardamom Shortbread

 An afternoon tea treat for cardamom lovers.

1/2 cup sugar	**Glaze:**
1 cup butter, room temperature	1 cup powdered sugar
1 teaspoon ground cardamom	1 tablespoon butter, melted
1 teaspoon vanilla extract	1 1/2 tablespoons brandy
2 1/2 cups flour	milk, to thin

Preheat oven to 325°. Grease a glass or nonstick 9 x 13 inch baking pan. In a large bowl, beat together sugar and butter until light and fluffy. Add cardamom and vanilla. Stir in flour. Press dough in baking pan. It works well to put a small plastic bag over your hand and press dough firmly into the pan. Bake for 20 to 30 minutes or until lightly browned.

While baking, prepare glaze. In a small bowl beat together powdered sugar, melted butter, and brandy. Add extra milk, 1 teaspoon at a time, to thin if necessary. Cut shortbread into small pieces while still warm. Drizzle with glaze.

Serves 20

Nutrition Information per serving:
Calories: 190 – Fat: 10 gm. – Protein: 2 gm.
Carbohydrate: 23 gm. – Cholesterol: 25 mg. – Fiber: 0

Carrot Cake

 Low fat, but fantastic. This may be the best carrot cake you have ever served and it is almost fat free. (Don't tell anyone!)

4 cups grated carrots (spooned, not packed into cup)	2 teaspoons vanilla
	2 cups flour
2 cups sugar	2 teaspoons baking soda
8-ounce can crushed pineapple, undrained	2 teaspoons cinnamon
1 cup prune puree or canned fruit purée*	1/2 teaspoon salt
4 large egg whites or 2 whole eggs	3/4 cup shredded coconut

Preheat oven to 375°. Grease a 9 x 13 inch baking pan. In a large bowl combine carrots, sugar, pineapple, prune purée, eggs, and vanilla; stir to blend thoroughly. Add remaining ingredients except coconut, and mix well. Gently stir in coconut. Spread batter in pan. Bake about 45 minutes or until pick inserted into center comes out clean. Cool on rack. Frost if desired.

*To make your own prune purée see page 210. The canned fruit puree may be used as a fat substitute in some recipes. It is usually found with the oils and shortenings in the grocery store.

Serves 16

Nutrition Information per serving:
Calories: 215 – Fat: 1 gm. – Protein: 3 gm.
Carbohydrate: 48 gm. – Cholesterol: 25 mg. – Fiber: low

Cherry and Apple Compote

 Serve on ice cream or frozen yogurt.

6 large tart apples, cored, peeled, and thinly
    sliced
2 cups (12 ounces) frozen pitted dark sweet
    cherries
1/4 cup lemon juice

1/4 cup honey
2 tablespoons brown sugar
2 tablespoons flour
1/2 teaspoon cinnamon
1/4 teaspoon nutmeg

Preheat oven to 350°. Butter a 1-quart casserole. In a large bowl, combine apples and cherries with lemon juice and honey. In a small custard cup combine brown sugar, flour, cinnamon, and nutmeg. Add to fruit and stir gently. Spoon into casserole. Cover and bake for 20 to 30 minutes or until apples are tender.

Serves 10

Nutrition Information per serving:
Calories: 115 – Fat: 0 gm. – Protein: 1 gm.
Carbohydrate: 28 gm. – Cholesterol: 0 mg. – Fiber: low

Chocolate Coconut Macaroons

 Chocolate and coconut—so good.

2 cups coconut

1/3 cup sugar

1/3 cup flour

1/4 teaspoon salt

1/4 teaspoon mace, optional

3 egg whites

1 1/2 teaspoons vanilla extract

2 ounces German chocolate squares

Preheat oven to 325°. Spray a nonstick baking pan with vegetable oil spray. In a large bowl, mix coconut, sugar, flour, salt, and mace. In a small bowl, lightly beat egg whites and vanilla with a fork or whisk. Stir into coconut mixture. In a small nonstick skillet, melt chocolate over lowest heat. Add to coconut mixture. Stir until well mixed. Drop by teaspoons onto baking sheet. Bake 10 to 15 minutes or until crisp around the edges. Watch carefully to prevent bottoms from burning. Cool immediately on wire racks.

Serves 30

Nutrition Information per serving:
Calories: 35 – Fat: 1.5 gm. – Protein: 0.5 gm.
Carbohydrate: 5 gm. – Cholesterol: 0 mg. – Fiber: low

Cinnamon Apple Slices

 A comforting, warm, healthy dessert with the aroma of apple pie.

5 large baking apples

1/4 cup apple juice

1/2 cup brown sugar

1/4 cup flour

1/2 tablespoon cinnamon

1/4 teaspoon nutmeg

1/4 teaspoon ginger

3 tablespoons butter or margarine

1/2 cup walnuts, chopped

Preheat oven to 350°. Grease a 9 x 9 inch or a 7 x 11 inch baking pan. Peel apples and cut each into 8 slices. Arrange apple slices in pan. Pour apple juice on top. In a small bowl, combine sugar, flour, cinnamon, nutmeg, and ginger. Add butter and cut into flour mixture with a knife or pastry blender until mixture resembles coarse cornmeal. Sprinkle evenly over apples. Top with nuts. Bake uncovered for 30 to 40 minutes or until apples are tender.

Note: Raisins can be substituted for the nuts.

Serves 6

Nutritional Information per serving:
Calories: 150 – Fat: 5 gm. – Protein: 1 gm.
Carbohydrate: 25 gm. – Cholesterol: 10 mg. – Fiber: medium

Coconut Macaroons

 If you love coconut, you will treasure this recipe! The nutmeg and mace make it unique. Check out the calories and fat—so low!

2 2/3 cups coconut (7 ounces)

2/3 cup sugar

1/3 cup flour

1/4 teaspoon salt

1/4 teaspoon mace, optional

1/4 teaspoon nutmeg

4 egg whites

1 teaspoon vanilla extract

2 tablespoons almond slivers

Preheat oven to 325°. Coat a nonstick baking sheet with vegetable oil spray. In a large bowl, mix coconut, sugar, flour, salt, mace, and nutmeg. In a small bowl, lightly beat egg whites and vanilla with a fork or whisk. Add to coconut mixture and stir with a spoon until well mixed. Drop by teaspoons onto baking sheet. Press together gently with fingers to form a ball. Press a piece of almond on top of each cookie. Bake for 10 to 12 minutes or until light brown on the edges and on the bottom. Do not overbake. Makes 36 small cookies.

Serves 36

Nutrition Information per serving:
Calories: 35 – Fat: 1 gm. – Protein: 1 gm.
Carbohydrate: 5 – Cholesterol: 0 mg. – Fiber: low

Cranberry, Apple, and Raspberry Custard Pie

 Beautiful and unusual fruit pie with a memorable taste of cinnamon and nutmeg. It is absolutely wonderful served either warm or cold.

1 cup sugar

1/4 cup brown sugar

2 tablespoons flour

3 eggs

1/2 cup evaporated fat-free milk

1/2 teaspoon allspice

1/2 teaspoon cinnamon

1/2 teaspoon nutmeg

1 cup cranberries

2 cups apples, peeled and thinly sliced in small pieces

1 1/2 cups raspberries, frozen in a bag (loose pack)

9-inch unbaked pie crust

Preheat oven to 425°. In a medium bowl combine sugars and flour. Add eggs, milk, allspice, cinnamon, and nutmeg. Beat well. Stir in cranberries, apples, and raspberries. Pour into unbaked pie crust. Bake for 10 minutes. Reduce oven temperature to 325°, cover loosely with aluminum foil, and bake 55 to 65 minutes or until custard is set and a knife inserted in the middle comes out clean.

Note: Fat-free half-and-half can be substituted for the evaporated fat-free milk.

Serves 8

Nutrition Information per serving:
Calories: 290 – Fat: 8 gm. – Protein: 5 gm.
Carbohydrate: 50 gm. – Cholesterol: 70 mg. – Fiber: medium

Cranberry-Oatmeal Chocolate Chip Cookies

 A winning combination of cranberries and chocolate!

3/4 cup shortening	1 teaspoon salt
1/2 cup sugar	1/2 teaspoon baking soda
1 cup brown sugar	1 1/4 cups flour
1 egg	2 cups quick-cooking oats
2 tablespoons milk	1 cup dried cranberries
1 tablespoon vanilla	1/2 cup chocolate chips

Preheat oven to 375°. Butter a cookie sheet. In a large bowl combine shortening, sugar, and brown sugar. Beat with electric mixer until creamy. Add egg and beat well. Add milk, vanilla, salt, and baking soda. Mix well. Stir in flour and oats. Stir in cranberries and chocolate chips. Drop dough by teaspoonfuls on cookie sheet. Bake for 10 to 12 minutes or until just lightly browned. Do not overbake. Cookies will appear soft. Cool 1 to 2 minutes on baking sheet. Remove cookies and cool on a rack. Makes about 3 dozen cookies.

Note: These cookies are also good without the chocolate chips.

Makes 36 cookies

Nutrition Information per cookie:
Calories: 110 – Fat: 5 gm. – Protein: 2 gm.
Carbohydrate: 14 gm. – Cholesterol: 5 mg. – Fiber: low

Fresh Peaches in Port Wine Sauce

 Sophisticated, simple, and so special!

2 cups port wine

1/4 cup sugar

1 stick cinnamon

8 medium peaches, peeled and sliced

In a small heavy saucepan, combine port wine, sugar, and cinnamon stick. Bring to a boil over medium heat and cook, stirring occasionally, 10 to 15 minutes or until mixture is reduced to about 1 cup. Remove from heat and remove cinnamon stick. Arrange peach slices in 4 small individual glass bowls or goblets. Spoon warm wine mixture over peaches.

Serves 4

Nutrition Information per serving:
Calories: 175 — Fat: 0 gm. – Protein: 1 gm.
Carbohydrate: 43 gm. – Cholesterol: 0 mg. – Fiber: medium

Ginger Cream Bars

 Wonderful blend of ginger, molasses, and lemon flavor.

1/2 cup vegetable shortening

1/3 cup molasses

3/4 cup brown sugar .

1 1/4 cups flour

1/4 teaspoon baking soda

1/2 teaspoon cinnamon

1/4 teaspoon ginger

1/4 teaspoon nutmeg

1 egg

1/2 cup toasted walnuts, chopped

Lemon Butter Frosting:

1 1/2 tablespoons butter, softened

1/2 teaspoon lemon zest

1 tablespoon lemon juice

1/2 teaspoon vanilla

2 cups powdered sugar

Preheat oven to 325°. Butter a 9 x 9 inch baking pan. In a small saucepan, combine shortening and molasses. Bring to a boil; remove from heat. Stir in brown sugar. Set aside. In a small bowl combine flour, baking soda, cinnamon, ginger, and nutmeg. Set aside. In a medium bowl, lightly beat egg. Add shortening and sugar mixture and beat with an electric mixer until light and fluffy. Stir in dry ingredients. Stir in nuts. Spoon mixture into baking pan. Bake for 25 minutes or until toothpick inserted in the middle comes out clean.

Prepare frosting: In a medium bowl combine butter, lemon zest, lemon juice, and vanilla. Add powdered sugar and beat with electric mixer until fluffy. Add more sugar if mixture is too thin. Spread on cooled bars.

Serves 16

Nutrition Information per serving:
Calories: 215 – Fat: 8 gm. – Protein: 2 gm.
Carbohydrate: 34 gm. – Cholesterol: 20 mg. – Fiber: low

Impossible Coconut Pie

 Crust forms on the bottom, custard appears in the middle, and coconut rises to the top. Impossible!

2 cups fat-free milk	1/2 cup flour
2/3 cup sugar	1/4 teaspoon nutmeg
4 eggs	1 teaspoon vanilla
1/4 teaspoon salt	1 cup coconut
1/2 cup butter or margarine	1 teaspoon freshly grated nutmeg

Preheat oven to 350°. Butter a 10-inch pie pan. Place all ingredients except coconut and 1 teaspoon nutmeg together in a blender or food processor. Process until well mixed. Stir coconut into the mixture. Pour into the pie pan. Top with nutmeg. Bake for 60 minutes. (If glass pan is used, lower temperature to 325°.)

Serves 8

Nutrition Information per serving:
Calories: 270 – Fat: 15 gm. – Protein: 6 gm.
Carbohydrate: 27 gm. – Cholesterol: 120 mg. – Fiber: low

Mystery Pecan Cheesecake

 A pecan pie and cheesecake combination, flavored with maple syrup and seasoned with allspice.

8 ounces fat-free cream cheese

1 egg

1/3 cup sugar

1 teaspoon vanilla

9-inch unbaked pie shell

1 cup pecan halves

2 eggs, lightly beaten

1/4 cup sugar

2/3 cup maple syrup

1/4 teaspoon allspice

1 teaspoon vanilla

Preheat oven to 375°. In small mixer bowl, beat together cream cheese, 1 egg, 1/3 cup sugar, and 1 teaspoon vanilla. Spread over bottom of unbaked pie shell. Arrange pecan halves on top of the cream cheese mixture. In a small bowl, combine 2 eggs, 1/4 cup sugar, maple syrup, allspice, and vanilla. Carefully pour over pecans. Bake for 40 to 45 minutes, or until set.

Serves 8

Nutrition Information per serving:
Calories: 320 – Fat: 12 gm. – Protein: 8 gm.
Carbohydrate: 45 gm. – Cholesterol: 70 mg. – Fiber: low

Oatmeal Cake with Coconut Nut Topping

 This homemade cake beats any packaged mix!

1 cup quick-cooking oatmeal

1 1/2 cups boiling water

1/2 cup butter or shortening

1 cup white sugar

1 cup brown sugar

2 eggs

1 teaspoon vanilla

1/2 teaspoon salt

1 teaspoon cinnamon

1/2 teaspoon nutmeg

1 teaspoon baking soda

1 1/2 cups flour

Topping:

1/3 cup butter, melted

3/4 cup brown sugar

3 tablespoons milk

1 cup coconut

1/2 cup walnuts, chopped and toasted

Preheat oven to 350°. Butter a 9 x 13 inch baking pan. In a small bowl combine oatmeal and water. Set aside. In a medium bowl cream butter and sugars. Add eggs and beat well. Add vanilla, salt, cinnamon, nutmeg, and baking soda. Mix well. Stir in flour. Stir in oatmeal. Pour into pan. Bake for 30 to 35 minutes. While cake is baking combine topping ingredients in a small saucepan. Bring to a boil over medium heat. Remove from heat. When cake is done, remove from oven. Change oven setting to broil. Spread topping on cake and place cake under the oven broiler. Broil 1 to 2 minutes or until topping is bubbly. Watch carefully to prevent burning.

Serves 16

Nutrition Information per serving:
Calories: 290 – Fat: 12 gm. – Protein: 3 gm.
Carbohydrate: 41 gm. – Cholesterol: 50 mg. – Fiber: low

Orange Poppy Seed Cheesecake

 Creamy, tasty, low-fat cheesecake. Is it possible? Try it or you won't believe it. This recipe was adapted from one that had 600 calories and 50 grams of fat per serving.

1 cup graham cracker crumbs	2 eggs
1/4 cup sugar	1/2 cup fat-free sour cream
3 tablespoons butter or margarine, melted	2 tablespoons orange juice
12 ounces Neufchatel cheese, room temperature	1 1/2 tablespoons grated orange rind
	2 teaspoons vanilla
1/2 cup sugar	1 tablespoon poppy seeds
1 tablespoon butter, softened	

Preheat oven to 300°. In a 9-inch pie pan, combine graham cracker crumbs and sugar. Add melted butter and stir with a fork until mixed well. Pat crumb mixture firmly into the pan. Set aside. In a medium bowl, combine Neufchatel cheese, sugar, butter, and eggs. Beat with electric mixer until smooth. Add sour cream, orange juice, orange rind, vanilla, and poppy seeds. Mix slowly just until blended. Pour into unbaked crust. Bake for 45 to 60 minutes or until lightly browned and set in the middle.

Serves 10

Nutrition Information per serving:
Calories: 250 – Fat: 14 gm. – Protein: 6 gm.
Carbohydrate: 25 gm. – Cholesterol: 75 mg. – Fiber: low

Pistachio Soy Delight

 This is a taste treat and you get some soy too!

1 package instant pistachio pudding mix

1/2 cup crushed pineapple

1 cup miniature marshmallows

12-ounce carton firm, low-fat tofu

1/2 teaspoon vanilla

1/2 cup chopped soy nuts or other toasted
    nuts, optional

Blend dry pudding mix, pineapple, marshmallows, tofu, and vanilla in food processor until smooth. Fold in chopped soy nuts.

Chill and serve with fresh fruit.

Serves 8

Nutrition Information per serving:
Calories: 100 – Fat: 1 gm. – Protein: 3 gm.
Carbohydrate: 19 – Cholesterol: 0 mg. – Fiber: medium

Pumpkin Cookies

 If you like a soft, moist, flavorful cookie, you will enjoy these pumpkin cookies. They keep well for several days but they will never last that long unless you hide them well.

1 1/3 cups butter or margarine	1/2 teaspoon baking soda
3/4 cup sugar	1/2 teaspoon salt
3/4 cup brown sugar	1 teaspoon cinnamon
2 eggs	1 teaspoon vanilla
15-ounce can pumpkin	1 cup chopped walnuts, toasted
3 cups flour	1/2 cup golden raisins, optional
1/2 teaspoon baking powder	1/4 cup coarse-ground decorative sugar

Preheat oven to 350°. Grease cookie sheet. In a large bowl beat butter, sugar, and brown sugar together. Add eggs and beat well. Add pumpkin and mix. Combine flour with baking powder, baking soda, salt, and cinnamon. Stir into batter. Add vanilla, nuts, and raisins. Drop batter by teaspoons onto cookie sheet. Sprinkle with sugar. Bake for 15 to 20 minutes or until set. Do not overbake. Remove from pan and cool on rack. Makes 60 cookies.

Serves 60

Nutrition Information per cookie:
Calories: 85 – Fat: 4 gm. – Protein: 1 gm.
Carbohydrate: 11 gm. – Cholesterol: 15 mg. – Fiber: low

Pumpkin Pie—Extra Smooth

 Add some soy to your life. It is so good and smooth.
No one will ever know this pie is made with tofu.

9-inch unbaked pie crust

15-ounce can pumpkin

12 ounces low-fat firm tofu

2 eggs, lightly beaten

1 cup sugar or 3/4 cup honey

1/4 teaspoon salt

1 1/2 teaspoons cinnamon

1/2 teaspoon ginger

1/4 teaspoon nutmeg

1/8 teaspoon cloves

Preheat oven to 350°. Press pie crust into 9-inch pie pan. Set aside. In a food processor combine all remaining ingredients. Process until smooth. Pour into unbaked crust. Bake for 50 to 60 minutes or until filling is set. Filling will appear soft but will become firmer as it chills.

Serve with light whipped cream.

Serves 8

Nutrition Information per serving:
Calories: 240 – Fat: 7 gm. – Protein: 6 gm.
Carbohydrate: 38 gm. – Cholesterol: 45 mg. – Fiber: low

Sour Cream Raisin Pie

 An old-time favorite with the warm taste of cinnamon and cloves.

3 eggs

1/2 cup white sugar

1/2 cup brown sugar

1/2 teaspoon salt

1/4 teaspoon cinnamon

1/4 teaspoon cloves

1/8 teaspoon nutmeg

1 teaspoon lemon zest, optional

1 1/2 cups low-fat sour cream

1 1/2 cups raisins

9-inch unbaked pie crust

Preheat oven to 450°. In a medium bowl beat eggs lightly. Add white sugar, brown sugar, salt, cinnamon, cloves, and nutmeg. Add lemon zest if desired. Mix well. Stir in sour cream and raisins. Pour into unbaked pie shell. Bake for 10 minutes, then reduce heat to 325°. Bake for additional 25 to 30 minutes.

Serves 8

Nutrition Information per serving:
Calories: 310 – Fat: 8 gm. – Protein: 5 gm.
Carbohydrate: 54 gm. – Cholesterol: 70 mg. – Fiber: medium

Southern Comfort Glazed Banana Cake

 Warm spices combined with warm Southern Comfort in a surprisingly moist cake.

1/2 cup vegetable oil

6-ounce jar baby food apricots

1/2 cup brown sugar

1/4 cup sugar

2 eggs

1 teaspoon vanilla extract

1 teaspoon baking powder

1/2 teaspoon baking soda

1 teaspoon salt

1/2 teaspoon cinnamon

1/8 teaspoon cardamom

1/4 teaspoon allspice

1/4 teaspoon nutmeg

1 1/2 cups flour

1/2 cup pecans, chopped

2 medium bananas, mashed

Frosting:

1 tablespoon butter or margarine

1 tablespoon milk

1 cup powdered sugar

1 tablespoon Southern Comfort

Preheat oven to 325°. Butter a 7 x 11 inch pan. In a large bowl beat together vegetable oil, apricots, brown sugar, and white sugar. Add eggs and beat well. Add vanilla, baking powder, baking soda, salt, cinnamon, cardamom, allspice, and nutmeg. Stir in flour. Stir in pecans and bananas. Pour batter into pan. Bake for 25 to 30 minutes or until lightly browned and cake springs back when lightly touched in the middle. Do not over-bake.

To prepare frosting combine butter and milk in a small saucepan. Heat over medium heat until butter melts. Remove from heat. Add powdered sugar and Southern Comfort. Beat until smooth. Drizzle warm frosting over cake.

Note: For a 9 x 13 inch pan make 1 1/2 times the recipe.

Serves 15

Nutrition Information per serving:
Calories: 220 – Fat: 10 gm. – Protein: 2 gm.
Carbohydrate: 31 gm. – Cholesterol: 25 mg. – Fiber: low

Spice Cake

 Super moist and super good. Soy flour is an extra bonus in this recipe, but regular flour can be substituted for the soy flour. This cake freezes well.

1 1/2 cups all-purpose flour	1/4 teaspoon allspice
1 cup soy flour or all-purpose flour	1/2 teaspoon nutmeg
2 cups sugar	1/3 cup soybean oil or other cooking oil
2 teaspoons baking soda	2 cups canned applesauce
1/2 teaspoon baking powder	4 eggs
1 teaspoon salt	1 cup raisins, optional
1 1/2 teaspoons cinnamon	1 cup toasted walnuts, chopped, optional
1/4 teaspoon cloves	

Preheat oven to 325° (or 300° if using a glass pan). Butter a 9 x 13 inch pan. In a large bowl, mix all the dry ingredients together with a spoon. Add oil and applesauce and beat with an electric mixer for 2 minutes on medium speed. Add eggs and beat 2 minutes. Stir in raisins and nuts. Pour into baking pan. Bake for 40 to 50 minutes or until cake surface springs back when touched lightly in the middle. If cake is browning too quickly on the bottom or sides, reduce oven temperature to 300°.

Serves 16

Nutrition Information per serving with raisins and nuts:
Calories: 290 – Fat: 8 gm. – Protein: 5 gm.
Carbohydrate: 50 gm. – Cholesterol: 50 mg. – Fiber: low

Nutritional Information per serving without raisins or nuts:
Calories: 245 – Fat: 7 gm. – Protein: 4 gm.
Carbohydrate: 42 gm. – Cholesterol: 50 mg. – Fiber: low

Stuffed Brandy Baked Apples

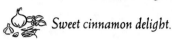 *Sweet cinnamon delight.*

6 large baking apples such as Granny Smith

1/2 cup flour

1/2 cup brown sugar

1/2 teaspoon cinnamon

1/2 teaspoon nutmeg

1 tablespoon lemon zest

1/4 cup butter or margarine

1/4 cup raisins or nuts

Topping:

1/4 cup brandy

1/4 cup cointreau or orange liqueur

1/4 cup water

1/2 cup low-fat whipped cream, optional

Preheat oven to 400°. Butter a 9 x 11 inch baking pan. Core apples. In a small bowl combine flour, brown sugar, cinnamon, nutmeg, and lemon zest. Cut butter into mixture using a knife or pastry blender until mixture looks like coarse cornmeal. Stir in raisins. Spoon mixture into the center of cored apples. Arrange apples in pan. In a small cup mix brandy, cointreau, and water. Pour over apples. Bake for 40 to 50 minutes or until apples are soft. Serve warm. Top with whipped cream if desired.

Serves 6

Nutrition Information per serving:

Calories: 270 – Fat: 8 gm. – Protein: 2 gm.

Carbohydrate: 47 gm. – Cholesterol: 25 mg. – Fiber: high

Index

CPSIA information can be obtained
at www.ICGtesting.com
Printed in the USA
FFOW02n1146220514
5490FF